THE AMBRIDGE BOOK
OF COUNTRY COOKING

Caroline Bone

THE AMBRIDGE BOOK OF COUNTRY COOKING

with illustrations by John Mansbridge

METHUEN
By arrangement with the British Broadcasting Corporation

First published in Great Britain 1986
by Methuen London Ltd
11 New Fetter Lane, London EC4P 4EE
Copyright © 1986 William Smethurst
Illustrations copyright © 1986 John Mansbridge
Printed in Great Britain

British Library Cataloguing in Publication Data
Smethurst, William
   The Ambridge book of country cooking.
   1. Cookery, International
   I. Title
   641.5   TX725.A1

ISBN 0-413-60440-3

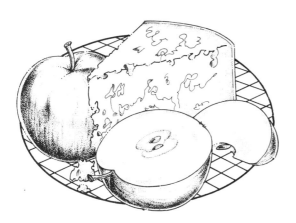

CONTENTS

Acknowledgements 6

January 7

February 19

March 33

April 47

May 59

June 71

July 83

August 95

September 107

October 121

November 133

December 145

Index 159

Acknowledgements

First and foremost I must thank my three friends from the Bristol wine bar days – Hedli, Julia, and Mary. Our venture into the restaurant business was not an overwhelming success, but we had great fun *cooking*, and devising our own recipes. Mary is now providing many of the dishes described in this book at the Three Ways Hotel, Mickleton, Gloucestershire.

The Borsetshire Farm Produce Council has collected many country recipes over the years, and I am grateful for the help and advice which they have so freely given. Mr Jack Woolley is not only the owner of Grey Gables but also of the *Borchester Echo*, and he has kindly allowed me to adapt traditional country recipes which were published in the *Echo* at the turn of the century.

Finally, I must thank the people of Ambridge itself, too numerous to mention by name, but all unfailingly generous in allowing me to use their favourite family recipes.

January

RECIPES FOR JANUARY

Lentil and rosemary soup

Nelson's chicken-liver pâté

Loxley leek and egg flan

A famous beef stew with prunes

Roasted guineafowl stuffed with grapes

Plough Monday pudding

Lord Netherbourne's brandied chocolate pots

Cinnamon buns

J A N U A R Y   N O T E B O O K

Snowdrops, delicate and frail, defy the frosts and the biting winds. In the hedgerows are the glowing red hips of the dog rose, black berries of ivy, and bright, brilliant beech leaves. In the hedgebottoms can be found the tiny, fresh green leaves of spring, and the flowers of red deadnettle and shepherd's purse. On a sheltered bank behind the coach-house a primrose unwisely opens a pale yellow eye to the wintry sun.

Two days of snow, a night of clear frost, and by morning birds flock round the bird-table in desperation. The blackbird still looks sleek and fat, the robin plump and cheery, but in truth they are having a hard time. Most birds, now, roost for fifteen dark hours and spend daylight in a weary search for food to get them through the next fifteen hours of night. Some birds have stored supplies against the winter. Coaltits and nut-hatches bury nuts in tree crevices and know where to go back and find them. Jays are even more cunning. They bury acorns and find them again by watching for the seed-lings to poke up through the soil. By the Am, goldfinches sway on hazel deadheads, plucking out seeds to eat.

Then more snow is whipped into huge drifts, and the following morning the village is cut off from the outside world. A JCB digger, hired by the County Council, starts clear-ing the Borchester road, working towards us from Edgeley. A group of schoolchildren climb Ten Elms Rise to see how far the digger has got – then spend the rest of the day tobogganing down Lakey Hill on blue plastic fertiliser bags. In the Bull at lunchtime Sid serves hot toddy and everybody is very excited, the commuters from Glebelands telling each other how ridiculous it would be to even *try* to get to work, and how their bosses will just have to put up with it. The milk tanker can't get through, and by the next morning the farmers' cooling tanks are overflowing. Milk is collected in a monster-size plastic bag and carried away across the fields on a tractor and trailer. A small group of virtuous sixth-formers plod after it, intent on catching a bus to school from Wharton's Garage. The rest of the children go back to their tobogganing on Lakey Hill.

At night foxes scream and bark, and hounds stir uneasily in their kennels. I always thought it was the dog fox that barked and the vixen that screamed, but Tom Forrest tells me both will bark and scream if the mood takes them. In the day it is Tom who prowls the boundaries of Leaders Wood and Lyttleton Covert, pondering over the tracks left in the snow. He shows me where several dog foxes have followed a vixen on heat, and where a playful fox has romped in the snow. Across the field is a single line of fox prints. 'Now, you might think that was a fox with two legs missing,' says Tom humorously, 'but it ain't. Charlie was having a romp in the snow when he spotted something to eat, and off he went, very fast, one foot *exactly* behind the other.' Foxes, he explained, have two methods of catching prey. If they come across grazing rabbits they dash into the middle, hoping to grab one that's either young and inexperienced or old and lame. But if they find a mouse or vole they sit and watch it for a bit, then jump in the air with a mighty leap and come down right on top of their victim, smacking it senseless with their nose.

Underground, oblivious to the clicketing of foxes, the huntsman's horn, or the laughter of village children, the mole pads along his runs gobbling up earthworms that have fallen through the roof. The more the ground freezes the deeper he must go, and the harder the ground will be to dig. But I have little sympathy. Moles are vicious and nasty. They eat each other, and when earthworms are plentiful they store them in secret caverns, first biting off their heads to stop them burrowing to safety.

RECIPES FOR JANUARY

Rosemary, they say, is for remembrance. It is an evergreen herb, its leaves thick and fresh even in the depths of winter. Passing the kitchen garden each morning, I crush a few leaves between my fingers and release a heady and reviving scent of lavender, pine, and the spiciness of ginger and nutmeg. There is many a wise old adage connected with the rosemary plant. When Pat and Tony moved to Bridge Farm they found a magnificent bush growing by the door, and were dismayed when it died almost instantly. 'Rosemary will never thrive,' said Tony's Grandma Perkins, firmly, 'near a house ruled by a woman.' Pat blinked several times and said: 'It died because Tony fell over it on his way home from the pub even though I'd told him a thousand times to fix the outside light. *And* he trampled over the cuttings I took. I really don't know why I bother.'

At Home Farm Brian is busy with early lambing. It still seems strange to see lambs shivering in the snow when they ought to be gambolling among the daffodils, but the early lamb, as Brian says, makes the highest price. He is out in the lambing sheds in all weather, and comes in at any time of the day or night for a sustaining bowl of thick, homemade soup. Jennifer takes pride in making sure it is ready for him. The rosemary bush outside *her* door is always green and vigorous, and she uses the fresh tips to add flavour to this heartwarming soup of potatoes and lentils.

Lentil and rosemary soup

1 lb red lentils
$\frac{1}{2}$ lb potatoes
3 pints light stock
1 3-inch sprig of fresh rosemary
2-3 pieces lemon skin
Freshly ground salt and pepper

In a large pan put the rinsed lentils and potatoes, scrubbed and diced. Add the stock and rosemary. Slowly bring to the boil, then simmer for 15 minutes. Add 2 or 3 pieces of lemon skin and continue simmering for another 15 minutes. Take out the lemon skin and rosemary and season to taste before serving. This is a thick, nourishing soup with a beautiful aromatic smell. It sets solid when cold.

(NB All recipes are for four people unless otherwise stated.)

At one time it was Jackie Woodstock who toiled over salads and quiches in the Wine Bar. 'Ah, where now are those pale, pale lips, that silvery ash-blonde hair?' sighs Nelson. 'That elusive smile, that knowing glance, that incredible recipe she had for baby scallops sautéed with avocado!' After Jackie came the lovely Lisa. 'Honey-blonde, honey-sweet!' cries Nelson as the memories flood back. 'Such warmth, such laughter, such wonderful lettuce soup!' Now there is Shane. 'Yes, well, he does become his butcher's apron better than any of them, don't you think?' Shane certainly thinks so. Two sad ladies from Waterley Cross sit in the window looking out at the slush and driving sleet. They have been to Underwoods' sale and are now eating Shane's sausage-meat plait. Nelson leans over to me and whispers, 'You are wise to choose my special chicken-liver pâté. It won first prize at Ambridge Fruit and Produce Show in 1979.' He adds, before I can spit it out, 'The recipe, of course. It belonged to Mrs P. I made Dad sneak into her cottage and steal it.' He smiles gently – and well he might, because it is indeed a most delicious pâté.

Nelson's (or Mrs Perkins's) chicken–liver pâté

1 lb chicken livers, cut into thin strips

4 oz butter

1 medium onion, finely chopped

2 cloves garlic, crushed

4 streaky bacon rashers, chopped

1 tablespoon cream or top of milk

1 tablespoon brandy

1 bay leaf (optional)

Heat the butter and cook the onion, garlic and bacon for 5 minutes. Remove with a slotted spoon. Turn up the heat and add the chicken livers to the butter. Cook until the outsides are sealed but the centres still pink. Put the chicken livers, bacon, onion and garlic into a liquidiser. Add the cream and brandy. Liquidise until smooth and turn out into a suitable pot or dish. If you wish, melt some extra butter and pour over the top. Place a bay leaf on the butter before it sets.

Higgs double-digs the vegetable plot this month, his constant companion a robin so tame it almost perches on his spade. He talks to it affectionately. The robin takes no notice. When Higgs sits down for a drink and a piece of cake (approximately every ten minutes), it waits for crumbs and Higgs asks its advice about his football pools or the 2.30 at Cheltenham. They both seem happy. Mr Woolley occasionally comes bustling by to ask if Higgs has ordered the seed potatoes yet, and why isn't he putting lime on the soil after digging, and is that really all the leeks and cabbages we have left? 'It wouldn't be all we had left,' says Higgs after some moments of thought, 'if you hadn't kept on eating them.' The garden does look very empty, and only half a row of leeks remain out of the six that were planted. Still, vegetables are for eating, and I ruthlessly demand some for a leek and egg flan I want to make.

I found the recipe in the *Loxley Cookbook*, a little book put together in aid of the Loxley Barratt church restoration fund. Now I like it so much – the leeks are so wonderfully juicy and the potato pastry so tasty – that I have promised to give Shane the recipe. He does *so* want to impress Nelson at the Wine Bar.

Loxley leek and egg flan

Rub the butter into the flour and then add the potatoes by pushing through a sieve with the back of a wooden spoon. Mix in thoroughly. When rolling this pastry out it is advisable to have lots of extra flour for your hands – it is much stickier than normal pastry. Line a 7-inch flan dish with the pastry and bake blind at 200°C (400°F, gas mark 6) for 10 minutes. While the pastry is cooking, sweat the leeks gently in the butter for about 5 minutes. When the base is ready spread the leeks over it. Beat the cream and eggs together with the seasoning and pour over the leeks. Cook at 180°C (350°F, gas mark 4) for 25 minutes, by which time the top will be starting to turn golden brown and the filling will be set.

Pastry

3 oz butter

4 oz self-raising flour

4 oz potatoes, boiled

Filling

8 oz leeks, split lengthways and cut into 1-inch lengths

1 oz butter

2 eggs, beaten

Freshly ground salt and pepper

$\frac{1}{4}$ pint single cream

A January dawn at Grange Farm. Eddie and the cows troop miserably into the milking parlour, Eddie huddled inside his donkey jacket with BCC (Borsetshire County Council) stencilled on the back. Half asleep, he doles out the dairy nuts, and takes the clusters off one cow to put on another. 'All right, off you go, Buttercup. Well come on, Lady Di, I haven't got all day.' Joe comes out, coughing in the raw morning air, and helps wipe down the cows' teats with a filthy rag. Eventually milking is over. They both go back to the kitchen and eat a huge breakfast of bacon and fried bread with pint mugs of tea. Then they slump on either side of the kitchen range and smoke cigarettes. When the post comes, Eddie reads the *Sun* and Joe mutters over the bills. 'The AI man wants his money fast enough. He ought to wait nine months till the calf arrives – ought to wait three years or more till it starts milking if there was any justice.' But there isn't any justice. 'Let's get moving,' says Eddie after a bit. 'Them cow cubicles have to be mucked out, we've been putting it off for three weeks.'

At dinner time, though, the world becomes a brighter, cheerful, infinitely more optimistic place. For a start there's only a bit of hedging and one more milking to be endured before a night at the Cat and Fiddle. And the dinner itself would cheer anybody up. Clarrie makes substantial country meals – liver and onions, stuffed lambs' hearts, steak puddings and chips – and she likes to try out new dishes whenever Joe and Eddie will let her. She found this recipe for 'a famous beef stew' in an old country cookery book, and served it up one day without mentioning that it contained juniper berries and prunes. Eddie and Joe both asked for second helpings, ate them, and then fell asleep. It's the highest form of praise that Clarrie knows.

A famous beef stew with prunes

2 lb beef, cut into bite-sized pieces
1 teaspoon juniper berries, crushed
1 small can of prunes
1 small can of stout

Put the beef and juniper berries in a casserole dish. Drain the prunes and add to the beef. Press them down with a spoon to break the skins and release the flesh. Cover with the stout (Clarrie normally uses Guinness). Put on a close-fitting lid and cook for 3 hours at 150°C (300°F, gas mark 2). During cooking you can give the mixture a stir to make sure the prunes have disintegrated into the liquid.

Twelfth Night, or the Feast of the Epiphany, lies at the heart of the old Christmas season that runs from Advent to Candlemas. It was a great medieval celebration, and up until the eighteenth century the custom of eating 'twelfth cake' was as common as pancakes are now on Shrove Tuesday. In Worcestershire farmers used to light fires in the sown wheatfields, and stand round them with their servants and labourers. Then they would all go to the cattle shed with a large plum cake (which had a hole in the centre) and they would wassail each ox, individually, by name, with flagons of cider. This custom confirmed Borsetshire farmers in their view that Worcestershire farmers were, one and all, as daft as brushes. In these parts farmers stayed indoors and drank cider, and their farm labourers did the same (if they had any cider) in their appalling hovels. They had little to celebrate. Soon it would be Plough Monday, and they would return to toil in the fields after their Christmas rest.

At Grey Gables, Mr Woolley wants a Twelfth Night party. He has read of the old custom of the bean cake. 'Everybody gets a slice, Caroline,' he explains, 'but only one man finds a bean in his bit, and he becomes King of the Bean and leads us all in merry revels. If it's a lady she'd be Queen of the Bean, of course.' 'What,' I ask, 'if it turns out to be Higgs?' 'Higgs won't be there, Caroline,' he replies. 'Not at £15.50 a ticket.' 'But if people have paid £15.50 a ticket they aren't going to want cake with beans in it, are they?' 'There's only one bean, Caroline, you haven't been listening,' says Mr Woolley reproachfully.

In the end we have a fancy dress dance, with a special Twelfth Night menu which features roast guineafowl stuffed with grapes and pistachio nuts. It is one of my favourite recipes. The meat is always tender and succulent and the gravy out of this world.

Roasted guineafowl stuffed with grapes

(serves 6 to 8 people)

2 guineafowl

2 lb seedless grapes

Half a bottle (or so) dry white wine

2-3 oz unsalted butter

4 oz hazelnuts

4 oz pistachio nuts

6 slices bacon, streaky or back

Tips of fresh rosemary

A few sprigs of parsley

Freshly ground salt and pepper

Watercress for garnish

Rinse the grapes and crush half of them in a large bowl. Put half the remaining whole grapes into the bowl. Add the nuts. Stir together. Stuff this mixture into the birds and truss securely. Brown the birds in 2-3 oz of butter and transfer to a casserole. Cover them with bacon. Add the wine and herbs. Roast at 200°C (400°F, gas mark 6) for 20 minutes. Add the rest of the grapes. Cover the birds with kitchen foil (or put secure lid on casserole) and cook for a further 40 minutes. Take off the foil, turn up the heat, remove the bacon, and allow the birds to brown nicely (5 minutes or so). Put the birds on a serving dish and garnish with watercress. The gravy can be served as it is, or reduced by boiling rapidly for a few minutes until it thickens. Take out the herbs before doing this and season to taste.

Plough Monday comes on the first Monday after 6 January, and it is still celebrated in Penny Hassett, where a plough decorated with green and yellow ribbons (representing grass and corn) is drawn through the village streets. Walter Gabriel remembers the Penny Hassett Plough Monday revels at the beginning of the century. 'The chaps who dragged the plough were called Plough Stots,' he told Mr Fletcher, who lives at Glebelands and is fascinated by tales of old country lore. 'And there was a chap dressed in women's clothes called the Betsey, and the Plough Stots and the Betsey would come and knock on your door asking for money, and when you gave it them they'd dance about crying, "Largesse! Largesse!" ' Mr Fletcher said: 'But what if you hadn't got any money for them?' 'Oh, they ploughed up your garden and made a horrible mess,' said Walter. 'Proper gangsters they was in Penny Hassett – still are, I daresay.'

This wonderful suet and plum jam pudding has been associated with Plough Monday for well over a hundred years.

Plough Monday pudding

6 oz self-raising flour
3 oz fresh wholemeal breadcrumbs
4 oz shredded suet
4 oz soft brown sugar
2 eggs, beaten
Milk to mix
Good red plum jam

Mix the flour, breadcrumbs, suet and sugar in a bowl. Add the eggs and enough milk to make a soft dropping consistency. Butter a 2-pint pudding basin and spoon some jam into the base. Build the pudding up with alternating layers of mixture and jam, finishing with pudding mix. Cover the bowl in the usual way with buttered greaseproof paper and foil. Leave a pleat across the top for the pudding to expand. Steam for 2 hours.

Lord Netherbourne, bless him, is my father's second cousin. He may even be once or twice removed, but I believe not. Anyway, he is certainly a Bone (actually, of course, not Bone but Bohun – we all came over with the Conqueror) and I have always called him 'Uncle'. Mr Woolley regards this as a valuable business asset, and tells the tale to Americans, Japanese, and Germans (the French just sneer and refuse to be impressed) whenever he can. 'The Bohuns are one of the oldest and most noble families in the kingdom,' he tells the business leaders of Osaka and Phoenix City. 'They're almost as old as the Woolhays. Have you seen the Woolhay Memorial in our little village church?' The business leaders are sometimes confused when he goes on to recount his childhood poverty in Stirchley, and how he clawed his way up by selling newspapers outside New Street Station, but they always treat me with a great deal of respect. Japanese have been known to bow to me, and Americans to jump to their feet every time I go into the dining room.

My 'uncle' came to dinner with me in January, and Mr Woolley was over the moon with delight. 'Did you enjoy your meal, Lord Netherbourne?' he asked loudly, for the benefit of a Bavarian tour operator at the next table, and 'Uncle' paused for a long moment before saying with infinite sadness: 'I was hoping there'd be a chocolate pudding on the menu, I *do* love a chocolate pudding.' Here is his very favourite.

Lord Netherbourne's brandied chocolate pots

4 oz plain chocolate
4 eggs, separated
2 oz sugar
2 tablespoons brandy
¼ pint double cream, lightly whipped

Melt the chocolate over a very low heat. Beat the egg yolks and sugar until pale and fluffy. Beat in the melted chocolate. Add the brandy. Fold in the lightly whipped cream. Fold in the stiffly beaten egg whites. Pour into individual dishes and freeze. Serve straight from the freezer.

A Martha Woodford recipe, this. She sometimes bakes a large batch of buns and sells them in the village shop, and I always buy a couple if I see them. They are moist, spicy, and fruity, and I have even seen children buying them in preference to sweets, which is praise indeed!

Cinnamon buns

½ lb self-raising flour
4 oz butter
3 oz soft brown sugar
1 tablespoon ground cinnamon
4 oz seedless raisins
2 oz chopped mixed peel
1 egg, beaten
1 or 2 dessertspoons milk

Sift the flour and cinnamon into a bowl. Rub in the butter. Add sugar, fruit and peel. Mix to a stiff batter with the egg and milk. On a well-buttered baking tray place about 12 heaps of the mixture. Bake for 15 minutes in a pre-heated oven 200°C (400°F, gas mark 6).

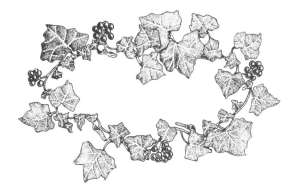

February

RECIPES FOR FEBRUARY

Colonel Danby's curried parsnip soup

Leek and parsnip soup

Baked leeks with prawns and walnuts

Bill Insley's cod and bacon supper

Lemon roast chicken with garlic

Game pie

Shula's pork chops in parcels

Toffee upside-down pudding

Wholewheat orange biscuits

FEBRUARY NOTEBOOK

Winter wheat pushes up through the powdered snow, a carpet of emerald green, and in the hedgerow are green shoots of honeysuckle and blossoms of green helibore. A mass of snowdrops, the 'fair maids of February', hang their delicate heads in the church-yard, while out on the hills the gorse is on fire with yellow flowers, and the first hazel catkins hang yellow on the bough. Catkins on the sallow are known as 'goose chicks' because they have the same soft, yellow-green colour and texture that goslings have when they are dry fom the egg.

It might seem the very depths of winter, with the sap at its lowest, and all nature either dead or sleeping, but the elder buds are bursting, daffodils grow an inch or more in a week, herons are building their nests by the lake, and badger cubs are already being born underground.

Rooks begin to return to the rookery in Leader's Wood. During the winter they have been to a communal roost many miles away, but now they too are thinking of spring. Rooks are too intelligent for my liking. Walking the old Roman road behind Home Farm I watch them at work repairing their nests, swooping and cawing and scolding and chattering to each other. Suddenly, for no obvious reason, there is a din of wild screeching and a pair of rooks quietly building their nest are descended upon and driven out by all the others. A few moments later and the nest has been destroyed, pulled to bits in a fury of destruction. What had the poor outcasts done? What law had they transgressed? Will they ever be permitted to return, and plead their case before a rook parliament?

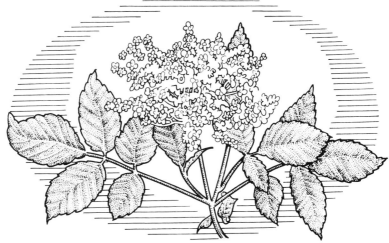

Starlings are also on the move, changing their roosting site and annoying Tom Forrest. They come down in a game covert and he tries desperately to move them on. He creeps out at dusk and fires a gun at them, waits for them to settle, then fires again. Still they return. He reads in his shooting magazine about a sophisticated ultrasonic noise-emitter that was developed by the Japanese for crowd control and has proved very effective against starlings roosting in Devon. Mr Woolley is not prepared to buy it, and treats Tom very severely. 'This isn't Tokyo, Tom,' he says, 'nor is it Torbay. You seem to be getting very cosmopolitan in your sunset years.' Tom is upset, not without reason. Starlings roosting by the thousand are a terrible nuisance. They break down branches and kill foliage with their mass of guano droppings. Every night dozens of them die of the cold and fall from their perches. Rats venture out to the forest floor to eat them, and then to burrow into the piles of droppings beneath the trees.

Another bird to annoy poor Tom is the bullfinch that visits his cottage each morning and strips the buds from Pru's ornamental forsythia. Tom is not allowed to shoot the bullfinch, because it is protected, but Pru is very distressed to see her forsythia being so ravaged, and when she is distressed she loses interest in cooking and Tom has a bad time of it. Personally I would rather look at the lovely bullfinch, with his pink breast and dove-grey back, than at the forsythia he nibbles.

RECIPES FOR FEBRUARY

February 'fill-dyke' they call it, but the dykes and ditches are usually brimming with melted snow rather than rain. The month that so often starts with crisp, frozen landscapes, azure skies, and glorious sunsets so often turns into a drear, damp, bone-chilling month of grey skies and mud. When he lived at Ambridge Hall the Colonel would watch anxiously as the swollen waters of the Am crept up the paddock until they lapped the wooden legs of Duckingham Palace itself. Lazy Mr Drake, though, would peer from his palatial abode and regard the flood water with satisfaction, a convenience designed to save him the trouble of waddling down to the river bank. He would plop straight down into the water, and the Colonel would return to the Hall, try to warm up the kitchen (the house is colder and damper than most) and make himself a ferociously spicy curried parsnip soup for lunch. The Colonel now lives in a bungalow at Manorfield Close, but he tells me that his memories of Mr Drake, and his recipe for soup, will remain with him always.

Colonel Danby's curried parsnip soup

Place the butter in a pan and heat gently. Add the parsnips (peeled and in chunks) together with the crushed garlic and chopped onion. Fry, stirring all the the time, for a couple of minutes; then lower the heat, put a lid on the pan, and cook for a further 10 minutes. Stir occasionally to stop the vegetables from browning. Add the curry powder and flour, then stir in the stock. Increase the heat and stir until it boils. Reduce the heat, put the lid on and simmer for 20 minutes or until the parsnips are soft. Cool and put through a blender (or a sieve if, like Colonel Danby, you don't have a blender!), then add salt and pepper and heat gently before serving. You can add cream and croutons, but Colonel Danby eats his with wholemeal bread and butter.

2 lb parsnips

1 onion, chopped

3 oz butter

1 clove garlic, skinned and crushed

1 level tablespoon flour

1 level tablespoon mild curry powder

2 pints stock

Freshly ground salt and pepper

This leek and parsnip soup is a great favourite of Richard Adamson, the vicar – and he very definitely likes a little bowl of croutons to sprinkle over the top. But then, he does have a wife to cook for him, and he knows the soup will be piping hot and the croutons nice and crisp when he returns home for lunch after a morning of parish visiting. Richard is a man who counts his blessings, and well he might when they include a wife like Dorothy and a soup like this.

Leek and parsnip soup

½ oz butter

1 tablespoon oil

1¼ lb trimmed leeks

1 lb parsnips

A generous pinch of oregano or mixed herbs

1 pint chicken stock

Freshly ground salt and pepper

½ pint semi-skimmed milk

Chopped parsley for garnish

Wash the leeks well and cut into ½-inch pieces. Thinly peel and slice the parsnips. Heat the butter and oil in a large pan. Add the leeks. Cover and cook, gently, for 10 minutes, taking care the leeks do not discolour. Add the parsnips, stock, and herbs. Bring to the boil. Cover. Simmer until the vegetables are tender (about 25 minutes). Cool a little and liquidise. Return to rinsed-out pan. Reheat and season to taste. Stir in ½ pint milk, or more if a thinner soup is desired. Heat gently and serve with chopped parsley and croutons.

(To make croutons cut 2 thick slices of bread into ½-inch cubes and fry in a little cooking oil or lard until golden brown. Drain on crumpled paper and serve in a dish.)

The leek was brought to England by the Romans, who prized it highly and believed it had medicinal properties. The Emperor Nero claimed that eating leeks helped to improve the sweetness of his voice and he ate so many that he was nicknamed 'Leekie' by the proletariat. In England the Saxons were so partial to leeks that the vegetable plot was known as the 'leac tun', and in Wales they embraced it as a national emblem.

Nowadays it is praised as being low in calories, high in Vitamin C and mineral salts, and a splendid source of fibre. Personally I love the taste and flavour, particularly in this super and rather sophisticated lunch dish. Carol Tregorran serves it with a mixed salad and a glass of her own Manor Court English wine. If you can't get hold of Manor Court (she says) try something like a Madeleine Angevine 1984 from the Astley Vineyard in Worcestershire.

Baked leeks with prawns and walnuts

Cook the potatoes and leeks together in lightly salted water until tender. Drain well. Mash with the butter and season to taste. Stir in the peeled prawns and chopped nuts. Either divide between 4 individual ovenproof dishes or place in a 2-pint shallow ovenproof dish. Top with breadcrumbs mixed with the cheese. Cook in a moderate oven at 190°C (375°F, gas mark 5) for about 25 minutes or until topping is slightly crisp.

1½ lb potatoes, peeled and quartered
1 lb trimmed leeks, cut into ½-inch slices
Freshly ground salt and pepper
1 oz butter
8 oz peeled cold-water prawns
2 oz walnuts, roughly chopped
4 oz brown breadcrumbs
2 oz cheddar cheese, grated
Unpeeled prawns, slices of lemon and parsley for garnish

'I just don't know what I'm going to do with that man,' says Martha fretfully, as retired Derbyshire farmer Bill Insley buys sausages, a tin of baked beans, a packet of powdered soup, a small white sliced loaf, and a packet of Turkish delight for his afters. 'He never seems to eat a proper home-cooked meal unless I ask him round to my little cottage, and I can't be doing that every night, can I, or folk will start to talk.' Neither Jill nor I reveal that folk in Ambridge started talking about her and Bill many moons ago (you have to be *very* discreet to keep a secret in Ambridge!).

A day or two later Martha does ask him to supper, and gives him Irish stew and apple crumble, and Bill asks her back to Willow Farm and says: 'Now for a real surprise – the Bill Insley gourmet special, frozen cod steaks with streaky bacon!' Martha eats to be polite, and is astonished to find that cod and bacon go together very well indeed. 'Why this is just the sort of thing my Joby would have liked!' she exclaims. 'Course he would,' grins Bill. 'Now, it's tinned tapioca for pud and I've run out of jam, but I daresay a spoonful of mango chutney'll slide down a treat, don't you?'

Bill Insley's cod and bacon supper

4 cod steaks
½ lb streaky bacon

Line a dish with half the bacon. Place the cod steaks on top. Cover the fish with the remaining bacon. Cook in a preheated oven at 220°C (425°F, gas mark 7). If the cod steaks are fresh 20 minutes ought to be enough, but frozen steaks will need about 30 minutes. Serve with green peas tossed in butter and lemon juice, and mashed potatoes.

(NOTE: The tapioca with mango chutney was just Bill's joke. His favourite sweet for any formal social occasion such as supper with Martha is mandarin orange segments decorated with whipped cream out of a tube and glacé cherries.)

They are getting ready for lambing at Brookfield. Every day now the ewes are given a special concentrate of rolled barley and soya bean to munch with their silage. In the middle of the month they are moved down to the cow pasture next to the farm buildings, and David starts to get the barn rigged-out as a vast maternity ward. I call round on an icy-cold Sunday morning and find him battling with straw bales and hurdles to make dozens of separate lambing pens. Sophie is helping, devastatingly lovely in her designer jeans and Cindy Thomson jumper, her cheeks coloured by the bitter wind and the effort of hauling desperately on a bale of straw while David shouts: 'Not *that* way, Sophie. Oh for Heaven's sake!' 'Sorry, David,' says Sophie, humbly, and I think it would be a good idea if somebody kicked David hard.

Sophie is also cooking lunch, and has to miss out on the gin-and-tonics while she gets things ready in the kitchen. Eventually we sit down to a wonderful lemon roast chicken with garlic followed by cherry pie. 'That wasn't bad at all,' says David sleepily, and he gets up and starts to lollop towards the sitting-room with its blazing log fire. 'You're not going to let her wash up!' I say, horrified. 'Lord, no,' says David. 'There's the dishwasher. You do know how to load the dishwasher, don't you, Sophie?' Sophie says she thinks so. I think somebody should kick David very hard indeed!

Lemon roast chicken with garlic

Clean the inside of the chicken and pack in the rosemary, garlic and lemon. Rub the chicken with the softened butter and season before roasting for 15 minutes per pound plus 30 minutes over at 220°C (425°F, gas mark 7) – or use roasting times for your own cooker. Serve with chicken juices poured over the meat.

1 chicken
4 or 5 sprigs of fresh rosemary
3 cloves garlic, peeled and cut into small pieces
1 lemon, cut into eight pieces
Softened butter
Freshly ground salt and pepper

It is more than sixty years since young Piggy Atkins, who was renowned for his ugliness, won the hand of the Ambridge beauty Rosemary Winyard and set himself up as a 'high-class family butcher' in Penny Hassett. His shop was the downstairs room of their tiny cottage, and for a while he and his bride lived in the one room over it, but by the time a little Piggy Atkins appeared on the scene ('Just as ugly as his dad,' remembers Walter Gabriel) and then a little Miss Piggy ('Lovely chestnut hair and big eyes like her Mum') they had saved enough to put down the deposit on a pleasant semi-detached villa. Piggy's son did even better during the war ('Like all butchers,' says Walter) and the present Piggy is renowned for his ugliness, which has come down intact through three generations, and for vast and ever-increasing wealth.

The butcher's shop in Penny Hassett, though, is surprisingly unchanged. In February there are rows of rabbits hanging over the window, and the last of the season's pheasants slung over hooks by the door. There are woodcock to be bought, skinned hares, and hand-raised pork pies. 'Local venison this week' says a chalked notice, and 'Pigeon breasts 30p each' says another, while a third tempts us with '3 brace of pheasants for your freezer, only £15'. In February a hot game pie is not only wonderfully rich and satisfying, it is surprisingly economical.

Game pie

2 lb mixed game (pheasant, rabbit, venison, pigeon, partridge)

1 or 2 onions, chopped

Seasoned flour

1 tablespoon oil

2 tablespoons butter

Freshly ground salt and pepper

Generous pinch dried thyme

A good puff pastry

Marinade

½ bottle red wine

2–3 bay leaves

12 juniper berries

2 tablespoons good oil

Celery leaves

2 cloves garlic, crushed

½ an orange

8 peppercorns

1 onion, cut in chunks

Marinate the game in an earthenware bowl for 24 to 48 hours, turning occasionally. Take out the meat and dry the joints with absorbent paper. Cut the meat into large chunks and toss in seasoned flour. Melt 1 table-spoon oil and 2 tablespoons butter in a large frying pan, and quickly fry the meat (in 2 or 3 batches if necessary) and remove to a pan or casserole. Fry the chopped onion, adding more oil and butter if necessary, until golden. Sprinkle with 2–3 tablespoons flour and cook, stirring, for a few minutes. Gradually add the strained marinade, stir till boiling, and add seasoning and a good sprinkling of thyme. Pour over meat, and add enough water to just cover. Bring to a simmer and cook in a slow oven at 150°C (300°F, gas mark 2) or simmer on top of the stove for 2–2½ hours. Leave to go cold (preferably overnight). Top with a good puff pastry and cook at 190°C (375°F, gas mark 5) for 30 minutes or until the pastry is golden brown.

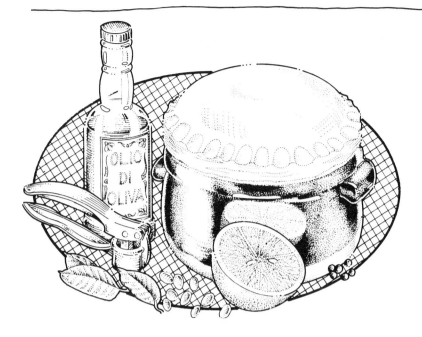

When Mark and Shula were first married they set up home in a beautiful flat in a Georgian house opposite the Old Woolmarket in Borchester. There they lived happily with their Habitat sofa and Laura Ashley curtains; their 'Design Centre' approved kitchenware and their coffee-maker; their microwave oven and remote-controlled television with video. In the evenings Mark would earnestly study his SDP policy pamphlets, and Shula earnestly study for her estate management exams, and then Shula would cook a delightful little supper with which they would drink half a bottle of wine; and after supper they would curl up on the sofa and listen to the beating of the February rain on the window, turn the central heating up a few degrees, and think how nice it was to be married, and how easy and pleasant life could be if only you were properly organised.

Elizabeth called them smug, self-satisfied and quite unbearable, but she did like dropping in for one of Shula's easily prepared but utterly delicious suppers – like pork chops in parcels. Mark does tend to whimper about the cholesterol levels involved, but both Shula and Elizabeth are country girls who know that butter and cream are good for you, and that Grandfather Dan, who lived to be almost ninety, ate two thick slices of fat bacon for breakfast almost every day of his life. 'I'm sure there's a time to ponder on saturated fats,' says Shula as she opens the foil parcels, 'but this isn't one of them.'

Shula's pork chops in parcels

4 thick pork chops or pork steaks	
1-2 ounces butter	
$\frac{1}{2}$ lb mushrooms, thinly sliced	
1 tablespoon flour	
Juice of 1 lemon	
Freshly ground pepper	
4 sprigs of fresh thyme	
$\frac{1}{4}$ pint double cream	

Trim excess fat from the pork and brown quickly in the butter. Remove and place on individual pieces of foil that are large enough to wrap them securely. Sprinkle with freshly ground pepper. Place a sprig of thyme on each chop. Fry the mushrooms in the butter for 2 minutes, then sprinkle in the flour and stir thoroughly. Add the lemon juice and mix in thoroughly for 1 minute. Divide the now congealed mushroom mix between the four chops. Pour two tablespoonfuls of cream over each chop and seal the parcels securely. Bake for an hour at 170°C (325°F, gas mark 3).

I was in the village shop, and Martha was telling me that her best-selling lines in February are always cough sweets and seed potatoes, when Joe Grundy came in and demanded both. 'A packet of Fisherman's Friends,' he said, 'and a bag of Arran Pilot.' Then he turned as white as a potato himself and gasped, 'They never cost that much!' Martha explained that Scotch seed potatoes are the best available, but Joe gave a bitter cry. 'English money! That's what the Scotch have always been after! My money! Money that ought to go in little William's money box!' He muttered and groaned by the birthday cards while Martha served me with golden syrup, honey and mixed dried fruit for a toffee upside-down pudding. But as I described the moist, spongy top, and the fruity, syrup-soaked base, Joe's features began to soften, and in a sort of absent-minded way he picked up a brown paper bag of Arran Pilot potatoes and drifted back to the counter. 'You'll have to give Clarrie the recipe for that pudd'n,' he said. 'It's just the sort of thing she makes for little Edward.'

Toffee upside-down pudding

Place a 7-inch cake tin over a gentle heat and melt 2 oz butter in it. Gradually stir in the golden syrup, sugar and honey. When it is mixed add the dried fruit. Remove from the heat and allow to cool while making the top.

To do this, cream together the butter and sugar. Then add the sifted flour alternately with the beaten eggs. Turn out on to the dried fruit mixture. Cook in preheated oven at 180°C (350°F, gas mark 4) for 20-25 minutes until the top is springy. Serve by turning upside down on a plate.

Base
2 oz butter
3 level tablespoons soft brown sugar
1 level tablespoon honey
3 level tablespoons golden syrup
4 oz dried fruit (mixed or to preference)

Top
2 oz butter
3 oz sugar
4 oz self-raising flour
2 eggs, beaten

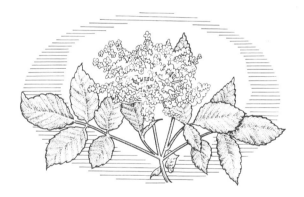

It was a wet, miserable afternoon, but Tom insisted on trudging round the game coverts scattering corn for his pheasants. 'It's a poor sort of keeper,' he said stoutly, buttoning up his old stalking jacket, 'who neglects his birds once the shooting season's over.' When he got back it was almost dark and he was shivering with cold, and when he got into his van the exhaust, which he had bashed against some packed snow three days earlier, promptly fell off. Poor Tom looked so miserable that I offered to run him home, and when he got to Keeper's Cottage he asked me in for a cup of tea.

Pru was in the kitchen and there was a warm smell of baking and the spicy tang of citrus fruits. 'You haven't gone and made your special orange biscuits!' said Tom, his face suddenly beaming with happiness. 'You must have known I was thinking about them all afternoon while I was feeding my birds!' Pru smiled at him fondly. She knows that when Tom isn't thinking of her orange biscuits he is thinking of her apple pies, her jam roly-poly puddings and her blackcurrant dumplings.

Wholewheat orange biscuits

8 oz wholewheat flour

4 oz demerara sugar

1 teaspoon vanilla essence

1 level teaspoon baking powder

4 oz butter

1 egg, beaten

Pinch of salt

Grated rind of 1 orange (or lemon if you prefer)

In a large bowl mix together the flour, orange rind, baking powder and salt. Then rub in the butter until the mixture is like fine breadcrumbs. Add the sugar. Add the vanilla essence. Add enough beaten egg to bind the mixture. Turn out on a floured board and knead gently. Roll the dough until it is half an inch thick. Cut into 2-inch rounds and place on a baking tray. Bake at 190°C (375°F, gas mark 5) for 10 minutes.

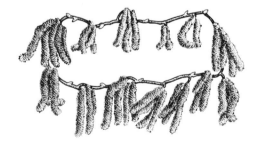

March

RECIPES FOR MARCH

Marjorie's marjoram casserole

Bacon soup with dumplings

Jethro Larkin's crisp-topped turnips

Pot-roast brisket with root vegetables

Duck roasted with wine and pears

Fillets of pork with apricots

Rhubarb and orange lattice tart

Rhubarb hot cake

Jill Archer's Sussex Pond pudding

MARCH NOTEBOOK

Daffodils, celandines, kingcups and dandelions are amongst the golden flowers of March. Mr Woolley knows a poem and recites it whenever a blackbird swoops past making its territorial war-cry. 'Oh blackbird, with your yellow, yellow beak,' calls Mr Woolley, 'you'd tell me why it's yellow, if only you could speak! And do you know what the blackbird says, Caroline?' 'No, Mr Woolley,' I say politely, and he goes on: 'I'll tell you why it's yellow, though I can only sing. I dipped it in a crocus on the first day of spring!'

Blackthorn bursts suddenly into blossom, a mass of creamy buds and white flowers, and there is a haze of new green along the hawthorn hedge. On some days the sky is a steely bright blue and the wind from the west comes sharp and penetrating. Tom shivers in his rather threadbare stalking jacket (Mr Woolley simply *must* buy him a new one!) and says that a March wind is an idle wind. 'Too lazy to go round you, so it cuts right through.' David Archer, though, says the March wind is the farmer's friend, breaking the frosted soil down into a friable seedbed. At the end of February he spread nitrogen over his yellowing winter wheat, and now it is shooting up again, a sea of emerald green.

For wildlife March is the hungriest month. Young grass is not yet growing, last year's herbage is withered and dry. Deer, rabbits and hares are hard put to find some of last year's bramble leaves, and squirrels have long since eaten the nuts they buried in autumn – or have forgotten where they left them! Tom and George kill grey squirrels using hoppers of poisoned corn ('Vermin!' says George, 'Tree rats!' says Tom) and voles and mice also eat the poisoned corn and are then eaten by barn owls (a protected species) who themselves rapidly die of the poison.

For the first time in my life I see March hares going mad! There are a dozen of them in the pasture next to Cuckoo Covert, chasing each behind the other in a circle. As I watch in amazement one of them suddenly stops, turns to face its pursuer, and soundly boxes its ears. 'That's what the doe does to the jack,' Tom tells me in the Bull later, 'to stop him getting too uppity.' Joe Grundy claims that Grange Farm hares play leapfrog games and hold regular boxing matches. 'If I've seen it once I've seen it a dozen times,' he insists. 'Me and Eddie've had wagers on who'd win.' Jethro says, 'That's what comes of drinking Cat and Fiddle beer at dinner time.' 'Oh no,' says Joe, 'I never saw any of them doing that.'

Joe tells us that toads are spawning in the pond at Grange Farm. 'It isn't commonly known that a toad's tongue faces backwards,' he says, and Tom says, 'Is that any toad, or just them as live at Grange Farm?' In March toads can travel up to half a mile from their winter hides to the water where they breed, moving by night in a long, laborious procession. If they cross a road many will be squashed, but they do not understand the danger because they are following the same route that toads have crawled along for hundreds of years.

RECIPES FOR MARCH

Marjorie Antrobus is worried about rooks that are still building nests in the dry, rotting branches of dead elm trees. 'Why on earth can't they realise that the elms are dead?' she demands, staring up at the cawing, raucous colony in Leader's Wood. But rooks, despite their fabled cleverness and cunning, are creatures of habit. Their exposed nests may be blown to shreds by the March winds, but they will not willingly move to oaks, limes, and pine trees even though Marjorie repeatedly advises them to do so. We go to Nightingale Farm to discuss a distribution rota for the parish magazine, and Marjorie points to the 'star recipe' in this month's issue. 'A great favourite of mine,' she says. 'I am sure that *everyone* is going to enjoy it.'

Marjorie's marjoram casserole

2 lb potatoes	
$\frac{1}{4}$ lb onions	
8 oz cheddar cheese	
2 or 3 tablespoons fresh marjoram, chopped	
Freshly ground salt and pepper	
16 oz bottled tomatoes (or a tin)	

Slice the potatoes and place a layer over the bottom of a buttered casserole dish. Put a layer of chopped onion, grated cheese, marjoram and chopped tomatoes over the potatoes. Add salt and pepper. Repeat in layers. Place a final layer of potatoes over the top. Cook for 2 to 3 hours at 170°C (325°F, gas mark 3).

On a biting cold morning I rouse Captain from his basket and drag him out for an invigorating walk. We watch thrushes prospecting for nests and in the woods we find the lovely blue and white flowers of the lesser periwinkle. By the Am we come across Joe Grundy and Eddie pollarding a willow. Eddie's face is red with effort as he lops off the branches, but poor Joe's fingers are blue with cold as he feebly tries to split them with a sort of primitive iron-age axe. 'Can't you do that another day?' I ask and Eddie shouts nastily, 'No he can't! We need fencing rails and he's too mean to buy them!' and Joe cries, 'It's the sap! The sap's rising and they'll never split!' Eddie swears at him, and Joe groans and shivers and casts an eye over Captain's new thermal dog coat.

I make my way to Grange Farm with a bag of jumble for the playgroup. Clarrie is making a huge pot of bacon soup with dumplings for lunch. 'I know they're in a terrible mood today,' she says, 'but if this doesn't cheer them up nothing will.'

Bacon soup with dumplings

---

2 pints water

---

1 lb soaked collar bacon joint

---

2 onions

---

1 parsnip

---

1 bay leaf

½ small white cabbage

---

4 carrots

Freshly ground salt and pepper

---

1 tablespoon tomato chutney

---

4 oz pork sausagemeat

---

4 oz self-raising flour

---

1 oz suet

Chopped parsley for garnish

Place the bacon in the cold water with the bay leaf, chopped carrots, sliced onions and chopped parsnip. Bring to the boil, cover and simmer for 40 minutes. Remove the bacon joint and chop into bite-size chunks. Return to the pan. Add finely shredded cabbage, seasoning and tomato chutney. In the meantime mix the flour into the sausagemeat, season and mix with the suet. Mix to a stiff dough with a little water. Divide into 8 or 10 balls and place on top of the boiling soup. Cover and simmer gently for a further 15 minutes. Serve garnished with chopped parsley.

(NOTE: a joint of smoked bacon is a delicious variation and can be used without soaking).

Jethro Larkin leans over the gate of Woodbine Cottage and talks to me about turnips. 'There was a prime minister called Turnip once,' he says. 'They called him Turnip because he was steady and reliable.' Recognising a fellow enthusiast, I wax lyrical about glazed baby turnips, and turnips in a cream sauce, and about the way turnips in casseroles absorb the flavours of other ingredients as well as imparting a sweetness all of their own. 'And have you tried stuffing turnips into a goose to help soak up the fatty juices?' I cry, and Jethro fixes me with a stern look. 'There's only one way I eat turnips,' he says severely, 'I cook 'em, I mash 'em, and I serve 'em up with a knob of butter and a shake of pepper. Not too much pepper, mind, otherwise it gets up Gyp's nose when I leave him a bit.' I tell Jethro that I'm sure he's quite right, but even so we must keep our minds open to new ideas, and I give him a recipe for crisp-topped turnips.

A week or two later I come across Clarrie gathering catkins with little William. 'My Dad never ceases to amaze me,' she says. 'He's been eating mashed turnip all his life and suddenly he starts demanding them with hardboiled eggs and Lancashire cheese. What's more, he says it's his favourite way of cooking them!'

Jethro Larkin's crisp-topped turnips

Ingredients
8 large white turnips
2 hardboiled eggs
2 oz fresh breadcrumbs
2 oz grated Lancashire cheese
2 oz butter
Chopped parsley for garnish

Peel the turnips and cut into large chunks. Cook in boiling water for about 10-15 minutes until tender. Drain well and toss in 1 oz melted butter. Turn into a pie dish. Fry the fresh crumbs in the other ounce of butter until light golden. Drain and mix with finely chopped hardboiled egg and grated cheese. Sprinkle over the top of the turnips and pop under a hot grill to crisp the top. Garnish with chopped parsley and serve.

This is the casserole to show the turnip at its superb and succulent best! Pot-roast brisket of beef with root vegetables – and the longer and slower the cooking the better it will be. Betty Tucker (who gave me the recipe) says that Mike prefers this to roast beef – and it's an awful lot cheaper! She believes the important thing is to give it plenty of time to cook, and eat it when the meat is so tender it falls away from the knife, and the gravy is rich and dark with beef juices and sweet vegetable flavours. Served up with creamed potatoes it will give total protection against cold March winds and driving March rain.

Pot-roast brisket with root vegetables

3 lb rolled brisket
4 carrots
5 small onions
3 turnips
4 sticks of celery
$\frac{1}{2}$ small swede
Vegetable oil or (if possible) beef dripping
$\frac{1}{2}$ lb flat mushrooms
$\frac{1}{2}$ pint rich stock
1 bay leaf
1 sprig of thyme
Freshly ground salt and pepper

Peel the turnips and swede and cut into chunks. Chop the carrots into large chunks and cut the celery into large pieces. Peel the onions but leave whole. Put the oil in a thick cooking casserole and heat. Sear and brown the joint. Take out, and put in the turnip, swede, carrots, celery and onion. Lightly brown, then remove. Empty the oil from the casserole, then put back the meat with the vegetables and mushrooms round it. Add the stock and the bay leaf and thyme. Season a little. Cover with foil and a tight lid and put back on the heat. Once the pot starts to simmer put in the centre of the oven, preheated to 140°C (275°F, gas mark 1). Cook for 4 hours.

All day Nelson had toiled in his father's garden, hoeing between the Green Windsor broad beans ('You has to move the soil every ten days, son,' called Walter, 'I'm moving it every ten minutes!' snapped Nelson); sowing parsnips, peas and radishes; lifting the last of the leeks to stop their growth ('You has to heel them in, son', 'I'll heel you in if you don't be quiet!'); and cutting brussels sprout tops to go with stuffed lambs hearts for supper. Late in the afternoon he finished his tasks, drank a cup of Walter's bright caramel-coloured tea, ate a slice of livid yellow-and-pink Battenberg cake, and fled to Grey Gables when Mrs Perkins came in demanding a game of ludo.

'It has been a day of unending horrors,' he confided over the cocktail bar. 'Come back to Borchester with me and have supper in the flat. We will drink champagne and talk of happy things.' 'Sorry, Nelson,' I said, remembering tales of his flat with its silver champagne bucket and black satin sheets. 'But if you need cheering up, why not stay here for supper? The duck's delicious – it's cooked with white wine, pears, and marmalade.' He looked at me reproachfully. 'I do not wish to cast out one nightmare,' he said, 'by replacing it with another. Duck with marmalade might seem the most haute of haute cuisine to Jack Woolley, but I would rather eat sprout tops that have been boiled for three-quarters of an hour because of Mrs Perkins's delicate digestion.' And off he went, which was a shame because duck with pears is *my* recipe, and I'm rather proud of it.

Duck roasted with wine and pears

Prick the skin of the duck, sprinkle with salt and pepper and roast in a fairly hot oven at 200°C (400°F, gas mark 6) for 20 minutes. Meanwhile, heat the marmalade, stock and wine until dissolved. Peel, core and quarter the pears, add to the marmalade liquid and simmer gently for 5 minutes. Drain off all the fat and juices from the duck and add the pears and liquor. Season well and return to the oven uncovered for 25 to 30 minutes, or until the duck is tender and well browned. Baste the meat once or twice during this time. Remove the duck and pears to a serving dish and keep warm. Spoon off any fat from the cooking juices, add the cornflour blended with the lemon juice, and bring back to the boil for 2 or 3 minutes. Spoon some sauce over the duck, and serve the remainder in a sauce boat. Garnish with watercress.

4 large duck portions

$\frac{1}{4}$ pint chicken stock

6 level tablespoons coarse-cut orange marmalade

$\frac{1}{4}$ pint white wine

1 lb firm Conference pears

2 tablespoons lemon juice

1 level tablespoon cornflour

Freshly ground salt and pepper

Watercress for garnish

I'll to thee a Simnell bring
'Gainst thou go'st a mothering,
So that, when she blesseth thee,
Half that blessing thou'lt give me

Robert Herrick

Mothering Sunday falls in the middle of Lent, and the old Borsetshire custom was that absent sons and daughters returned home on that day bearing flowers and Simnel cakes, and the entire family sat down to a dinner of roast pork. The custom died out, alas, in the nineteenth century, and the modern 'Mother's Day' owes more to the enthusiastic efforts of greeting card manufacturers and florists than to an upsurge in traditional feelings. But we do have a special Mothering Sunday service at St Stephen's, and for those who like to be traditional but different at the same time, here's a very tasty way to cook pork fillets.

Fillets of pork with apricots

4 oz dried apricots

2 tablespoons dry sherry

2 pork fillets

Lightly seasoned flour

1 oz butter

2 tablespoons brandy

4 tablespoons sour cream

Freshly ground black pepper

Lemon juice

Cover the apricots with water and soak for 4 hours. Add the sherry, bring to the boil and simmer for 15 minutes. Strain and reserve both fruit and liquid. Trim and skin the fillets. Slice them, and toss them in the flour. Sauté in the melted butter until golden brown. Drain off the excess fat. Heat the brandy and pour over the pork once it has been ignited. Add the apricots and stir. Pour the sour cream into the apricot liquid, then add both to the pan. Simmer for a minute or two, then season with black pepper and a little lemon juice.

At the end of every cottage garden, often in the spot where they kept the pig in days gone by, there now grow luxuriant, leafy vegetables with regal names like Prince Albert and Victoria Pale. 'They're called that because the Old Queen was very partial to rhubarb,' Tom told me, as he peered under an up-ended plastic bucket at the first pink, tender shoots of spring. 'Do you know, she had more rhubarb varieties named after her than roses? Nobody ever ate rhubarb till she took it up – but when the Queen started eating it everybody had to.' 'I didn't,' said Walter Gabriel, huddled in his overcoat and casting envious eyes at Tom's celery trench. 'Couldn't stand the stuff when I was a nipper, and what's more I don't remember Queen Victoria eating it either.' Tom said, 'There's no need to be argumentative, she could have eaten it while you weren't looking.' Walter said, 'Doh! I remembers the funeral cortège leaving Windsor right enough.'

Anyway, the new season's rhubarb is now available either under buckets or in the shops, and rhubarb and orange tart is very popular in the restaurant at Grey Gables.

Rhubarb and orange lattice tart

Preheat the oven to 220°C (425°F, gas mark 7). Sift the flour and icing sugar into a bowl, and rub in the butter until the mixture resembles fine breadcrumbs. Mix to a firm dough with water. Roll out and line an 8-inch ovenproof plate, saving the trimmings for the lattice. Chill. Cut the rhubarb into 1-inch lengths and put on the pastry. In a basin, blend the sugar, flour, egg and orange rind. Put orange juice into a measuring jug, make up to $\frac{1}{4}$ pint with cold water. Pour into a pan, bring to boil, and then pour on to the flour mixture. Stir briskly. Return to the pan and bring to the boil, stirring all the time. Pour over the rhubarb. Cut pastry trimmings into strips and form a lattice pattern over the top. Bake for about 35 to 40 minutes. Serve hot or cold.

Pastry
6 oz plain flour
1 oz icing sugar
3 oz butter
2 tablespoons water

Filling
1 lb early rhubarb
6 oz sugar
1 oz flour
1 egg, beaten
Grated rind of 1 orange
2 tablespoons orange juice
Cold water

It was Mrs Perkins who told me about rhubarb cake. 'It's what the farmers used to eat on Lady Day,' she said, 'after they'd paid their rents and had a glass of sherry with the squire.' I said what a wonderful recipe it would make for the parish magazine, but Mrs Perkins cannot abide Marjorie Antrobus, so I went round to Nightingale Farm and handed it over myself. 'I'll try to squeeze it in,' said Marjorie. 'Mrs P. is so keen to help me, bless her. But the most interesting thing anyone can do with rhubarb is to grow it as an ornamental shrub in the herbaceous border. The variety Stockbridge Arrow has the most beautiful bright red stems imaginable.'

Rhubarb hot cake

(serves 6 to 8)

8 oz self-raising flour

Pinch of salt

Generous pinch of nutmeg

1 oz butter

1 oz sugar

1 egg, lightly beaten

$\frac{1}{4}$ pint milk

Filling

8 oz chopped rhubarb

2 oz sugar

$\frac{1}{2}$ oz butter

Sieve the flour and salt together and stir in the nutmeg. Rub in butter to the fine breadcrumb stage. Add the sugar. Mix in the egg and enough milk to make a soft dough. Divide the mixture in half and roll out into 2 rounds about 7 inches across. Place the first ring on a baking sheet, cover with rhubarb mixed with sugar, and dot with butter. Divide the second ring into 6 or 8 wedges and place these over the rhubarb. Bake in the oven at 190°C (375°F, gas mark 5) for about 40 minutes. Dust with icing sugar and serve straight away with extra stewed rhubarb.

Phil Archer's favourite pudding gets its name from the lemony, buttery sauce that streams out of the suet case when it is cut and forms a pond in the pudding dish. In the heart of the rich but feather-light suet there nestles a whole lemon, which some experts say ought to be cut into segments and served on each plate. But Phil does not want bits of lemon, nor does he want the addition of currants and sultanas (as Jill, in a foolish, frivolous mood, once tried). What he wants is a large slice of suet crust pastry with lemon-soaked base, a large spoonful of sauce, and plenty of custard or cream.

Jill Archer's Sussex Pond pudding

Reserve a quarter of the pastry (see below), and line a buttered 2-pint pudding basin with the rest. Press the cuts firmly to seal. Grate the butter and put half of it, together with half the sugar, into the basin. Prick the lemon all over and put that too into the basin. Cover with the rest of the grated butter and sugar. The basin needs to be full. Wet the pastry edges, fit the reserved pastry as a lid, and seal well. Cover with buttered greaseproof paper and foil, and steam for 2 hours, adding more boiling water as necessary to maintain the level. Turn the pudding out on a shallow dish, and cut open at the table.

8 oz suet crust pastry
4 oz butter
4 oz demerara sugar
1 large, thin-skinned lemon

Special suet crust pastry

8 oz self-raising flour

3 oz suet

2 oz butter, chilled and grated

1 egg, beaten with a little water

1 oz demerara or soft brown sugar

Grated lemon rind to taste

Mix the flour and the fats and the lemon rind. Stir the sugar into the egg. Make a well in the flour mix and add the egg and sugar. Bring together with a fork, then roll out and use as directed.

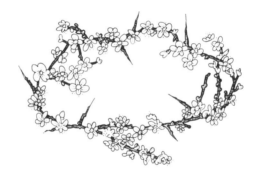

April

RECIPES FOR APRIL

Plaice with egg and prawn sauce

Spring salad

Gammon steaks with sour cream and cucumber

Jersey bean crock

The Colonel's lambs' kidneys with redcurrant jelly

Baked carrot pudding

Brandied orange cider syllabub

Treacle tart

APRIL NOTEBOOK

Dog violets and primroses open in the hedgerows, the water meadow is bright yellow with dandelions and nodding cowslips, and bees murmur in the white blossoms of the wild cherry. Along the edge of Leader's Wood bloom wild daffodils (they call them Lent Lilies in these parts) and behind the pale, creamy daffodils the woodland rides are covered in a vast carpet of wood anemones and bluebells.

I am at Brookfield one evening when David comes home with a dozen day-old ducklings, twelve little balls of fluff in a cardboard shoebox. He has been to talk to a farmer in Loxley Barratt about borrowing the potato harvester, and the farmer's daughter has fallen madly in love with him (so he says) and has given him the ducklings to remember her by. Sophie looks at him, stunned, and blinks several times. 'You do know he's making it up, don't you,' says Jill, gently. Sophie says, 'Oh yes, I mean, well *of course* . . . ' but she still looks at the ducklings doubtfully. Elizabeth comes in from a hard day at Borchester Tech. 'I don't know if you've noticed,' she says, 'but the lowest bough on the brushwood sheaf is breaking out into tiny leaf.' Sophie says, 'You've made up a poem! Oh Elizabeth, you are clever!'

Later, I help David and Sophie put the ducklings under a broody hen. We creep out to the hen-house and carefully, in pitch dark, raise the lid of a nesting box. 'We just have to take the pot eggs away, and slip them gently under her,' says David, 'and in the morning she'll think she's hatched twelve little ducks.' 'Poor hen,' says Sophie, 'it's not her fault she isn't very bright.'

This is the month for birdsong. Skylarks wheel and sing over the cornfields; orchards are full of the calls of greenfinches and blackbirds. Great tits, robins, and tiny wrens pipe up in the hedgerows, and each evening Jennifer goes to Leader's Wood to listen to a nightingale. It is the song thrush, though, perched up on the topmost branch of the apple tree, his speckled front shining in the spring sunshine, who outsings them all.

Birds have reason to feel pleased. Nature has conspired to provide everything they need for the nursery and the larder. Foliage spreads out to shelter their egg-filled nests, while the leaves of oak trees are covered in millions of little green caterpillars, just waiting to be fed to young birds. There are flying insects and worms, while succulent fruit buds are clearly intended as appetising morsels for the bullfinch. Pru Forrest has

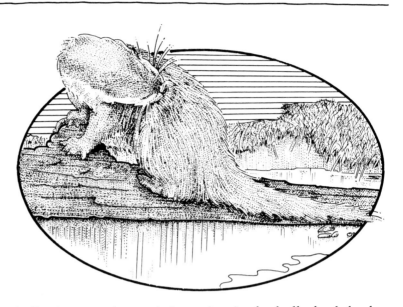

been feeding a blackbird all winter, and now it is nesting in the holly bush by her kitchen window, and is so tame that it will accept crumbs from her hand.

Other birds, also, are in search of food. Crows and jays feast on baby blue-tits and infant robins. I hate crows, and ask Tom why he doesn't go out and shoot some instead of messing about killing squirrels all day. 'It's no use you getting sentimental about blue-tits,' he says in his robust countryman's voice, 'they have nine or ten fledglings every year. The world would be swarming with them if something didn't happen to put things right.'

R E C I P E S   F O R   A P R I L

In April an otter and her cubs were living on the stretch of water between Grange Farm and Grey Gables. 'Tarka of the Am!' proclaimed Mr Woolley, proudly. 'Spot the Ot' said the Grundies – and they had more right to give it a name because the otter's 'holt' was on their bank of the river. Spot (or Tarka) lived on the harvest of the deep (brown trout and eels captured in four feet of muddy water), and one day I saw a kingfisher dart under the bridge and emerge with a small silvery fish in her mouth.

Neither kingfisher nor otter demanded that their food be served in exciting new ways, with exotic sauces, which was just as well because traditional country cooking is far from brilliant when it comes to fish recipes. Ambridge is a long way from the sea, and most folk, sadly, would as soon eat frogs' legs in aspic as they would delicious monkfish, red mullet, or fresh grilled sardines. During the winter we have lobsters brought up from Cornwall by lorry, and serve poached scallops with a vanilla sauce, but in April, when the scallops are over and the new season's crab has not yet arrived, a favourite fish dish in the restaurant is fillet of plaice with egg and prawn sauce.

Plaice with egg and prawn sauce

4 fillets of plaice
4 eggs, hardboiled and roughly chopped
8 oz cold-water prawns, cooked
$\frac{3}{4}$ pint milk
$1\frac{1}{2}$ oz plain flour
$1\frac{1}{2}$ oz butter
Freshly ground salt and pepper
Chopped parsley for garnish

Place the fish in a saucepan and pour on enough milk to cover. Bring to the boil and simmer gently for about 5 minutes until the fish is firm. When ready put on one side and keep warm. Return the hot milk used for the fish to the rest of the $\frac{3}{4}$ pint, and add more to make up the full measure if necessary. Melt the butter, then stir in the flour and cook for a minute, stirring all the time. Carefully add the milk (also stirring all the time!) and cook for 5 minutes. Add the eggs and prawns and heat through. Season as necessary and pour over the fish. Sprinkle with the chopped parsley and serve with creamed potatoes and peas.

With spring in the air and the sap rising, I begin to long for summer salads and the fresher, crunchier textures of picnics and late suppers *al fresco*. But in April, the gardens can still only offer the increasingly tired winter vegetables we have been using for many months, and there is little to herald the glories of summer fruits and vegetables. One alternative is this tasty spring salad which I served to Shula one splendidly peaceful lunch time recently, with a glass of white wine, some of Jean Paul's delicious fresh lunch rolls, and the windows of my sitting room flung open wide to the sunshine over Grey Gables' gardens.

Spring salad

2 apples (1 red and 1 green), cored and chopped
2 large carrots, scrubbed and chopped
1 head of celery, washed and chopped
3 oz walnut halves
1 tablespoon mixed fresh chives and parsley, chopped
Sour cream
Lettuce leaves for serving

Line an attractive salad bowl with the lettuce leaves. Combine the apple, celery, carrot, nuts and herbs in a large bowl. Pour over the sour cream and mix thoroughly to make sure that everything is coated. Pile the salad on to the lettuce leaves and serve immediately. For a less luxurious version, a lemon- or orange-flavoured dressing can be used instead.

'There are few things in this life,' said George Barford, crouched next to me and peering down into the clear, celandine-fringed water of a woodland pool, 'half as interesting as the love life of the newt.' 'Really, George?' I said, fascinated. 'Newts do not jostle and barge about while courting,' he continued solemnly. 'Oh no, the male newt wins the affection of his loved one by floating up and down in front of her. Then he flicks his tail and she is thrown head-over-heels backwards.' We watched for newts a while longer, but they were shy and hid themselves in the weeds, so we walked down to the village. George wanted his dinner and I wanted a word with Christine about our three-day riding holidays.

When we went in she was cooking gammon steaks under the grill, and furiously slicing up cucumber. 'Gammon is George's favourite,' she said, 'but I get so fed up with the eternal pineapple rings and tomatoes. Goodness only knows what he'll make of this.' George sat down at the table, the plate was put in front of him – on it a thick gammon steak covered in cucumber sauce and sprinkled lavishly with parsley. He took a large mouthful and chewed carefully. He frowned. Then he spoke. 'The way a female newt wraps her eggs in bits of water plant to protect them is blooming marvellous,' he said.

'What about your lunch, George?' asked Chris, a touch peevishly. 'Isn't that blooming marvellous?' 'Oh aye,' said George, 'but I often wonder why you don't cook gammon with parsley sauce. That's how we always have it in Yorkshire.'

Gammon steaks with sour cream and cucumber

Heat the butter in a large pan. Stir in the flour. Cook for 1 minute. Gradually stir in the stock, then the sour cream. Add lemon juice, garlic, seasoning and mustard. Cook, stirring, for 3 minutes. Add the sliced cucumber. Stir the mixture well. Cover and simmer for about 20 minutes, or until the cucumber is tender. Stir from time to time. Meanwhile, snip the fat round the edges of the gammon, and brush the surfaces with oil. Grill. Arrange the steaks on a hot serving plate. Spoon cucumber sauce over and garnish with chopped parsley.

4 gammon steaks
2 cucumbers, sliced
1 oz butter
1 oz flour
$\frac{1}{2}$ pint chicken stock
$\frac{1}{4}$ pint sour cream
Juice of $\frac{1}{2}$ lemon
1 clove garlic, crushed
2 teaspoons made English mustard
Freshly ground salt and pepper
A little oil

Tony Archer does not find it easy to express the warmth and loving regard he undoubtedly feels towards his sisters. Few can detect the gruff affection when he calls Jennifer 'that pain in the backside' or Lilian 'that Jersey cow'. In the spring, Lilian (who is fabulously rich and owns half the farms in Ambridge, including Tony's) came home from the Channel Islands and asked Pat and Tony out for dinner at Redgate Manor Country House Hotel. Astonished, Pat murmured, 'Oh, we couldn't possibly – you *must* come and have supper with us,' and Lilian said, 'Oh all right, restaurants are so boring, aren't they?'

After her supper at Bridge Farm, Lilian said, 'I almost forgot, I've got a present for you,' and handed over a brown paper bag before disappearing off into the night. Tony peered eagerly into the bag. His eyes popped with fury. 'Beans!' he gasped. 'She's given us a bag of beans!' They poured them out on to the kitchen table. There were dried broad beans, and runner beans, and black-eyed beans, and red kidney beans, and beans neither of them could hope to identify.

'I suppose I've got to plant them,' railed Tony, stomping up and down the kitchen, 'and wait for a magic beanstalk and climb up it and grab hold of the giant's naked houri . . .' Pat said, coldly, 'Hen, Tony. The giant didn't have a houri, or a cellar full of lager, he had a hen that laid golden eggs. And these must be Jersey beans – they're for making a special casserole that Jennifer's been raving about for weeks.'

Well, Jersey crock is a wonderful, thick, rich, warming casserole, and worth any number of meals at pretentious Redgate Manor. It's ideal if you can use genuine Jersey mixed beans, but otherwise just select whatever beans you can get from your local healthfood shop.

Jersey bean crock

1 lb mixed beans
1 pork hock
1 onion, roughly chopped
Chicken stock, as required

Rinse the beans and put them in a saucepan. Cover with plenty of water, bring to the boil for 2 minutes, then leave to soak overnight. In the morning drain and rinse them in a colander and then put them in a casserole dish and mix in the onion. Make a nest in the middle of the beans for the hock, then cover everything with chicken stock. Make sure the lid is close-fitting and put the casserole in the oven at 150°C (300°F, gas mark 2) at 9.00 am. Check a couple of times during the day in case the stock needs topping up. It will be ready to eat at 7.00 pm.

(NOTE: Originally, in Jersey, this dish used to be taken to the baker's in a pot 'crock' to be cooked all day in the bread ovens. It is delicious eaten with French bread and lots of cider.)

The Colonel is passionately fond of kidneys. He devours them on toast with mushrooms, he devils them at every opportunity, and he adores them served 'in pyjamas' – sliced with their circle of fat still on them, then fried till the fat is golden and crisp but the kidneys are still pink in the middle. But when a celebration is in order (the Queen's birthday, Freddie's birthday, Mrs Perkins's birthday, Mr Drake's birthday) he has a very special kidney dish indeed.

I called in at Manorfield Close with an invitation for him to play golf with Mr Woolley, and found him swathed in his butcher's apron, busy with the sliced kidneys, the port wine, and the redcurrant jelly. 'Whose birthday is it today?' I enquired, and he looked a trifle sheepish. 'Not exactly a *birthday* my dear – but the anniversary of the gallant defence of St Foy by Colonel Burton and the second battalion the 60th foot – 28 April 1760, you'll recall.' I had to confess that I didn't, and the Colonel looked rather severe. 'To those whose regiments go back to the old 28th, the old 48th, and the second battalion the old 60th, it is a date that can never be forgotten. Open a bottle of wine and join me for supper, there's a good girl.'

The Colonel's lambs' kidneys with redcurrant jelly

While melting the butter in a pan, skin, core and slice the kidneys. Cook, keeping them on the move until they are sealed. Remove from the pan and keep warm. Add the spring onion to the juices in the pan and cook for one minute. Stir in the flour and stock until you have a creamy sauce. Season, then add the mustard, redcurrant jelly and sherry. When this is satisfactorily blended, return the kidneys to the sauce and reheat for a few moments (without boiling!).

16 lambs' kidneys
$\frac{1}{4}$ pint dark stock
1 oz butter
1 spring onion, finely chopped
$\frac{3}{4}$ oz plain flour
1 tablespoon made mustard
2 teaspoons redcurrant jelly
2 tablespoons medium dry sherry
Freshly ground pepper

The WI monthly competition was for the 'most unusual' pudding, and poor Mrs Perkins was in a terrible state. 'I do a nice barley pudding,' she told me outside Martha's. 'Is a barley pudding unusual, do you think?' I said I thought it sounded *quite* unusual, and we went inside to buy some barley flakes. Martha didn't have any. '*I'm* going to make a pineapple upside-down pudding,' she said, 'I think they're ever so unusual.' 'No they're not,' said Mrs Perkins. 'You always make pineapple upside-down pudding. You made one for the "most interesting" pudding competition last March.' 'Well, I'm sure I don't know,' said Martha in a huff.

Outside again, I gave Mrs Perkins the recipe for my friend Mary's special baked carrot pudding, which can be eaten hot or cold and has the most delicious filling imaginable. Mrs Perkins looked dubious. 'We ate a lot of carrot cakes and puddings in the war,' she said. 'Not like this,' I assured her. 'This has got melted butter, and brandy, and egg yolks and cream.' She made it, and it won first prize!

Baked carrot pudding

8 oz sweet shortcrust pastry
(see next page)

Filling

2 oz finely grated carrot

2 oz breadcrumbs

1 egg white

2 oz melted butter

1 liqueur glass of brandy

1 tablespoon orange-flower water

2 egg yolks

$\frac{1}{4}$ pint cream

3-4 tablespoons sugar

$\frac{1}{2}$ teaspoon nutmeg

Line an 8-inch tart tin (that has a removable base) with pastry. Beat the filling ingredients together, adding sugar and nutmeg to taste. If you haven't any orange-flower water, it can be bought from a chemist, or add a little extra cream and nutmeg. Bake at 180°C (350°F, gas mark 4) – or a slightly lower temperature, depending on your oven – until the filling has risen and acquired a golden crust. Eat warm or cold.

Jean Paul's shortcrust pastry

Rub the butter into the flour until it resembles breadcrumbs. Stir the sugar (if used) into the beaten egg. Pour the egg into the flour and butter and mix until a firm consistency is achieved. Wrap in a polythene bag and chill in the fridge for half an hour before use. Roll out on a floured surface and use as required. (Always remember to take it out of the fridge a little before you need it, otherwise it will be too hard to roll.)

8 oz self-raising flour
5 oz butter
1 largish egg, beaten
1 tablespoon brown sugar, if pastry is to be sweet

'The easiest things are the wickedest things,' said John Tregorran, bearing a silver tray of crystal-cut glasses filled with syllabub into the dining room at Manor Court. 'This is true in cooking,' he said, placing them carefully on the dark-oak William and Mary gateleg table, 'and it is double true of life itself.' Carol gave him a quiet, tolerant smile.

John is a romantic. He came to Ambridge as a young man (living in a green horse-drawn caravan) and wooed her passionately for many years. Now he is a sweet but rather staid lecturer on English period furniture – but he still wears his hair artistically long, favours large floppy bow ties, and likes to say obliquely interesting things.

Personally, I do not find it at all easy to be wicked. I have wished, at times, that I did, so that wickedness would be more fun than it was. But I have no problems enjoying John's wickedly creamy and alcoholic syllabub.

Brandied orange cider syllabub

Mix together the cider, orange juice, orange rind, brandy and caster sugar in a large bowl. Cover and leave to stand for at least 3 hours. Stir from time to time. Add the cream and whisk well until the mixture forms into soft peaks. Put into 4 individual glasses. Do not put back into the fridge before serving, or the cold might cause the mixture to separate.

4 tablespoons medium cider
2 teaspoons finely grated orange rind
2 tablespoons orange juice
2 tablespoons brandy
$1\frac{1}{2}$ oz caster sugar
$\frac{1}{2}$ pint fresh double cream

They were out potato-planting at Brookfield, Jethro driving the tractor and Betty Tucker and Dorothy Adamson perched behind him on the planter, dropping the seed potatoes down the chute and singing 'Fly me to the Moon' in loud cheery voices. Potato-planting is the only time of the year they use casual labour at Brookfield – much to Jethro's relief. He feels very uncomfortable driving his tractor with Mrs Vicar and Betty Tucker bawling their heads off behind him, and when they shriek things like 'In other words, hold my hand. In other words, darling, kiss me' his ears turn red and one can tell that he is muttering 'My eye!' over and over to himself.

At dinner time he retires to the machinery shed with his sandwiches, and Dorothy and Betty go into the kitchen where Jill (because they are visitors) feeds them up on lamb stew and treacle tart. That doesn't please Jethro much, either – he's very fond of Jill's treacle tart.

Treacle tart

Pastry
8 oz self-raising flour
5 oz butter
1 egg, beaten
1 tablespoon brown sugar
Filling
1 tablespoon ground semolina
5-6 heaped tablespoons golden syrup
2-3 heaped tablespoons fresh wholemeal breadcrumbs
Juice of an orange
1 teaspoon finely grated lemon rind

Make the pastry in the usual way and line a well greased 7-inch flan dish, reserving the trimmings. Prick with a fork and sprinkle semolina over the base. Heat the golden syrup gently and stir in the breadcrumbs until you achieve the consistency you like (I prefer a moist centre, but others like it more firm). Add the orange juice and lemon rind and pour into the pastry case. With the remaining pieces of pastry make a lattice pattern on top of the tart. Bake at 200°C (400°F, gas mark 6) for about 25 minutes. Serve warm.

May

RECIPES FOR MAY

Buttered salmon steaks in white wine

Borsetshire cheese and crab soup

Sugar-browned new potatoes

New potatoes in lemon sauce

Chicken-liver and green peppercorn pâté

Deep-fried stuffed mushrooms

Rosemary roast lamb with onion and apple sauce

Elizabethan pork hot-pot

Christine Barford's cinnamon gooseberry pie

Spiced bread-and-butter pudding

MAY NOTEBOOK

The hawthorn hedge that runs down to the river by Ambridge Farm is weighed low with creamy blossom, filled with Betty Tucker's bees feasting on the sweetness within. Betty will soon have combs of delicately flavoured honey to sell with her milk round, and in the autumn the hedge will be a mass of crimson hawthorn berries.

Bluebells are now in full splendour carpeting the woodland floor, and cowslips and wild primroses cover the old turf meadows. Along the verges are the tiny white flowers of Jack-by-the-hedge and the purple and yellow of heartsease, and along the banks of the Am are ragged robin and pink cuckoo flowers – which open, so Borsetshire tradition would have us believe, when the cuckoo itself sings without stammering. At Grey Gables the chestnuts are opening out their magnificent clusters of white flowers, and the undergrowth by the lake is filled with the scent of wild garlic.

Tom comes into the shop, a cheery smile on his face. 'I've just seen a hedgehog courting his lady love, Martha,' he says, 'and it's a very remarkable sight!' Martha says, 'Oh yes?' in a warning tone, just in case Tom is going to be smutty. 'The female curls herself up,' says Tom, 'and the male runs round and round her in circles. It's a rare thing to catch sight of, I can tell you.' 'No it isn't,' says Joe Grundy, lurking, as inexplicably as ever, by the birthday cards. 'They're always doing it at Grange Farm. Scampering about like nobody's business.'

Martha has always been saddened by the mating of the stickleback. At this time of year, she tells us, the male stickleback goes bright red and builds a watery nest out of river weed, then dances and twirls in front of passing females until he entices one of them into his nest to lay her eggs. After that she swims away and leaves him to bring up the family. 'I cried and cried about that,' says Martha, 'when I was a little girl.' Joe says that family life is a most important thing, and Tom tells us about midges. 'D'you know why clouds of midges on a May evening won't bite you? It's because they're male midges waiting for the females to come out, and male midges don't bite.' Joe says, 'All midges bite at Grange Farm.'

Badger cubs can be seen in the early evening, playing near the entrance to their sett. They roll over each other, puff out their fur the way a cat does its tail, and in their excitement occasionally let off a dreadful pong from their musk glands. Fox cubs play in broad daylight. The vixen cubbed in March, and now the young are ready to be weaned. They are getting big and boisterous and a nuisance to her, so she leaves them to frolic in the sun all day, and returns only when it is time to feed them.

RECIPES FOR MAY

'The finest salmon,' Mr Woolley confidently tells a group of American tourists, 'comes from the icy-cold waters of the green Atlantic, and has been caught as it enters a river in the Western Isles.' The tourists, who are, like the salmon, the first of the season, look at Mr Woolley with respect. 'It's a question of oil and flesh,' Mr Woolley adds kindly, as he quotes chunks out of Jennifer's article in last week's *Echo*. 'Once upon a time,' he goes on with a merry laugh, 'it cost a penny a pound and the brave 'prentice lads o' London would eat it three times a week!' The guests chuckle nervously, clearly more confused than when they returned from watching *The Winter's Tale* at Stratford. There are no complaints, though, after they have eaten our special salmon steaks poached in wine and served with lightly cooked cucumber.

Buttered salmon steaks in white wine

Wipe the steaks. Melt half the butter. Grease a dish and place the salmon in it. Pour the melted butter over the top. Add the juice of half a lemon. Add the wine. Cover and put in a moderate oven, 180°C (350°F, gas mark 4), for 30-40 minutes. In the meantime dice and peel the cucumber and simmer in a little salted water until tender. Drain. Add the rest of the butter and plenty of pepper. Serve the salmon with the cucumber and garnish with watercress.

4 salmon steaks
$\frac{1}{2}$ lemon
$\frac{1}{4}$ pint dry white wine
1 cucumber
4 oz butter
Freshly ground salt and pepper
Watercress for garnish

Traditional Borsetshire cheese is, alas, like Dorset Blue Vinney, very hard to come by. Walter Gabriel can remember 'rounds' of it being produced by farmers down in the Vale, and sold on stalls at Borchester Market, but nowadays there are only one or two specialist shops that stock the genuine article. Traditional Borsetshire was a double-curd cheese (one batch of curds was made in the evening, and added to freshly made curds next morning) and was rich and creamy with a piquant flavour. The modern Borset-shire, however, is a single-curd cheese and is white, crumbly and mild. It is superb for toasting and excellent for adding to cooked dishes – which is why I always use it in this light, delicious, cheese and crab soup. Even single-curd Borsetshire cheese is some-times hard to come by, and I find that Lancashire cheese makes a reasonable substitute.

Borsetshire cheese and crab soup

2 oz butter
1 small onion, finely chopped
2 oz plain flour
1¾ pints chicken stock
5 oz white crab meat
4 oz Borsetshire or Lancashire cheese, crumbled
Freshly ground salt and pepper
Chopped chives for garnish

Melt the butter in a saucepan. Add the onion, then cook gently until soft but not browned. Add the flour, stirring constantly, and pour in the stock, still stirring. Bring to the boil, then simmer for 5 minutes. Put the crab meat and crumbled cheese into a liquidiser. Add enough soup liquid to moisten the ingredients and reduce them to a smooth purée. Add the purée to the pan, simmer gently for 5 minutes, season, and garnish with chopped chives.

Higgs's hand slides gently down into the warm, peaty earth. It feels around, delicately, for some moments. On Higgs's cunning face is a look of terrible greed. Suddenly the hand pops up out of the earth – and in it is a shiny white potato the size of a pigeon's egg! The earliest of early English potatoes are not in the shops until late in the month, but at Grey Gables Higgs grows his own supply in pots in the greenhouse. They are not, I hasten to add, for the enjoyment of the guests in the restaurant, but for Higgs and his widow-woman friend from Hollerton to gobble up in Higgs's flat over the stables. One morning I found Mr Woolley pleading for a handful to give the Admiral for lunch, but Higgs just stared into the middle distance with a face of stone. The widow woman demands to be pampered with many treats and luxuries, and it was Mr Woolley, after all, who stopped him taking her for joy-rides in the Bentley.

Here are two delicious ways to serve baby new potatoes – although the very earliest, of course, need nothing more than a dab of butter and a touch of black pepper.

Sugar-browned new potatoes

Plunge the potatoes into boiling, salted water. Bring back to the boil. Simmer for 10-20 minutes depending on size. Drain. Melt the butter and sugar in the pan. Add the potatoes and toss over and over until they are golden brown.

1 lb new potatoes, scraped
1 teaspoon of salt
1 oz butter
1 oz white sugar

New potatoes in lemon sauce

Make the sauce by melting the butter, adding the flour, and cooking for one minute. Add the stock, then the milk, stirring all the time until the sauce is smooth. Add the lemon rind, lemon juice, sugar, salt, pepper and the lightly boiled potatoes to the pan. Continue to simmer for 8 minutes or so. Just before serving add the cream. Garnish with chopped parsley.

$\frac{1}{2}$ oz butter
$\frac{1}{2}$ oz flour
$\frac{1}{4}$ pint milk
$\frac{1}{4}$ pint chicken stock
Rind of a lemon
Juice of half a lemon
1 teaspoon sugar
Freshly ground salt and pepper
1 lb new potatoes, lightly boiled
1 tablespoon single cream
Chopped parsley for garnish

Shula's blue mini races along the lane past Bridge Farm and Ten Elms Rise, then past the turning to Brookfield ('My poor car can't understand why we don't turn in at the farm gate' says Shula) and then on to St Stephen's church, and the small, mellow, brick-built cottage she inherited when her grandfather died. Every evening Mark is busy laying a path down through the vegetable plot to his newly started compost heap, watched, he says, by an affronted blackbird in the old lilac tree, and Shula is busy painting and decorating inside the cottage. ('I'll never sand another floor,' she vows, 'or rub down another pine door as long as I live'). When they have finished they either go for a late supper at Brookfield, or come up to Grey Gables for a bar snack. Mark has developed a distinct craving for our chicken-liver and green peppercorn pâté. Sometimes he eats it with hot granary toast, and sometimes inside deep-fried stuffed mushrooms, which we serve with home-made mayonnaise mixed with finely chopped cucumber.

Chicken-liver and green peppercorn pâté

1 lb chicken livers
$\frac{1}{2}$ lb butter, softened
1-2 cloves garlic, crushed
$\frac{1}{2}$ onions
$\frac{1}{2}$ teaspoon nutmeg
$\frac{1}{2}$ teaspoon ground cloves
1 tablespoon brandy
1 tablespoon French mustard
Freshly ground salt and pepper
2 tablespoons green peppercorns

Cover livers with salted water, bring to the boil and simmer for 15-20 minutes. Drain. Put into a blender. Add the remaining ingredients, except for the peppercorns. Blend until smooth. Line a loaf tin with cling-film and pour in enough melted butter to cover the bottom. Sprinkle with the green peppercorns. Put in fridge to set. Pour the pâté mixture over it. Chill, and keep for a few days before serving.

Deep-fried stuffed mushrooms

1 lb large button mushrooms
A little butter
6-8 oz chicken-liver and green peppercorn pâté
Flour
Beaten egg
Breadcrumbs

Remove the stalks from the mushrooms. Take a small, sharp knife and scrape out the insides of the mushrooms. Fry the trimmings with a little butter and mix into the pâté. Fill each cavity with the pâté. Dust each filled mushroom with flour, dip in beaten egg, and roll in homemade breadcrumbs. (If you put your breadcrumbs on a baking tray in a low oven to dry out, and then re-blend them, they will make a better coating.) Leave the mushrooms for an hour before deep frying. Serve with home-made mayonnaise to which some finely chopped cucumber has been added.

Jennifer has a cade lamb all of her own, the last of the Home Farm orphans, born too late to be fostered or exchanged through the farmers' lamb bank. Instead it spent its first tottering days in the cool oven of the Aga, and now trots round behind her on strong woolly legs. 'Brian hates hand-reared lambs,' says Jennifer sadly. 'Just because they creep up behind people, then rush forward and bowl them over. It's only their sense of fun.' Brian says, 'They just want food, that's all.' Jennifer's cade lamb was fed first on expensive cow's milk, but now it can be given cheap powdered milk and weaned on to grass. When I called round at Home Farm it was tethered to a collar and line in the orchard and Brian was viewing it with a more tolerant eye. 'I'll give her a bit of corn in a month or two,' he murmured, 'and by autumn she'll be fattened up nicely for the deep freeze.'

Jennifer's lamb at least has the summer ahead. This year's January-born lambs are now in the shops, and there is no taste to compare with young Hassett lamb roasted with rosemary, the leg served pink and succulent and the shoulder served with a crisp brown skin and accompanied by a special onion and apple sauce, as below.

Rosemary roast lamb

Stab the skin to allow the fat to escape, then cover with the sprigs of rosemary. The shoulder needs to be fairly well cooked to release the fat from the joint. Start in a hot oven for 20 minutes at 230°C (450°F, gas mark 8), then turn down to 180°C (350°F, gas mark 4) for 35 minutes per pound.

1 shoulder of lamb
Sprigs of fresh rosemary

Onion and apple sauce

Peel and slice the apples and onions. Melt the butter in a frying pan and add apples, onions, sugar and salt. Cover the pan and simmer gently, stirring occasionally, until the onions and apples are tender. When soft, turn the mixture into a serving bowl and serve hot with shoulder of lamb. (This is also delicious with goose or duck.)

4 large onions
2 Bramley's seedling apples
2 oz butter
1 oz sugar
Salt to taste

'I haven't tasted this,' said Joe Grundy, 'since my Susan passed on to a better place. It was my grandma's recipe, and she got it from her grandma before her. Was that one of them guineafowls yowling?' he added, and I said I thought the yowling was just little William playing Red Indians. Joe looked relieved. 'Guineafowls give a terrible yowl when they've laid an egg,' he said, 'and that's how you find their nests. Listen for a yowl, then head in the opposite direction, because they're all ventriloquists. Now this recipe came down, through the family, from the Grundies in the time of Good Queen Bess. Sir Walter Grundy got it from the Queen herself, according to my old granny, so you take care of it.' I took the piece of tattered paper, and thanked him.

Later, back at Grey Gables, Tom told me that Joe was quite right about guineafowl crying out when they laid an egg, and about them throwing their voices to evade detection – so perhaps he was telling the truth about Sir Walter Grundy as well! I tried his grandma's recipe for Elizabethan pork hot-pot, and found it wonderful, although here I have added curry powder and changed the inevitable cider into red wine.

Elizabethan pork hot-pot

2 lb boned shoulder of pork
A little oil and butter for frying
1 large onion
$1\frac{1}{2}$ tablespoons flour
$\frac{1}{2}$ lemon and $\frac{1}{2}$ orange
2 cooking apples
1 head of celery
$\frac{1}{2}$ teaspoon curry powder
2 oz raisins, 2 oz dates and 2 oz walnuts
Fresh sweet herbs (marjoram, basil and oregano)
$\frac{1}{2}$ teaspoon nutmeg
1 tablespoon honey
Red wine as required

In a heavy flame-proof casserole, fry the cubed meat quickly in a little oil and butter. Remove the meat and gently fry the sliced onion till golden. Replace the meat and sprinkle with flour. Add grated lemon and orange rind and the fruit segments. Add peeled and chopped apple, chopped celery, fruits, nuts, spices and a handful of fresh marjoram, basil and oregano (or half the amount of dried herbs) together with honey and freshly ground salt and pepper. Mix well. Add enough wine to barely cover the ingredients, bring to a simmer, cover and cook in a low oven at 150°C (300°F, gas mark 2) for $2\frac{1}{2}$-3 hours.

Rhubarb comes first in the season, but rhubarb is a vegetable; the first fruits of the year are hard green gooseberries, and a green gooseberry sauce is delicious with roast pork. To make it, cook $\frac{1}{2}$ lb hard, cooking gooseberries and a handful of sorrel leaves in water, drain and sieve, add a large nob of butter and a shake of nutmeg, and season with salt and black pepper. If you dislike a sharp sauce add a little sugar.

Gooseberry tart is an old favourite, especially when served with sweetened whipped-cream, but I am partial to this gooseberry pie with cinnamon, which was contributed to an Ambridge WI recipe book by Christine Barford in 1947. 'I was seventeen and I'd just left school,' she told me, 'and I made this pie for Jack and Phil one Saturday when Mum and Dad were away at a farm sale. We'd done the recipe in Domestic Science but I didn't put enough sugar in, and the pastry was awful, and the gooseberries were only half cooked, and Jack refused to eat it. I cried, and Phil ate two helpings just to cheer me up. Then he had stomache-ache all evening.'

Christine Barford's cinnamon gooseberry pie

Mix the berries, sugar and cinnamon together and place in a pie dish. Leave to stand for a little while and then stir well. Add the water. Roll out the pastry until it is slightly larger than the top of the pie dish. Trim off a border $\frac{3}{4}$ inch wide. Dampen the edge of the pie dish, and line with the pastry border. Dampen this pastry and place the remaining sheet of pastry over the dish. Trim, seal the edges well, and shape with a knife. Use the pastry trimmings to decorate the top. Stand on a baking sheet and cook in a hot oven at 220°C (425°F, gas mark 7) for 15 minutes, or until pastry is a light brown. Reduce heat to 180°C (350°F, gas mark 4) and cook for another 30 minutes. Sprinkle with caster sugar.

8 oz shortcrust pastry (see page 57)

2 lb hard green cooking goose-berries, topped and tailed

6 oz sugar (or to taste)

2 level teaspoons cinnamon

1 tablespoon water

Caster sugar

Mike Tucker leaned against his milk van, drank the mug of coffee Betty had brought out for him, and said, 'I'm a bread-and-butter man. I don't like fancy grub or fancy folk. I'm like them there guinea pigs.' 'The guinea pigs,' said Betty, after a moment's thought, 'never meet any fancy folk to speak of.' 'They've just met Caroline here,' said Mike, and I said, 'Yes, and they liked me very much!' The two guinea pigs, which belong to Brenda and Roy, were in a wire-netting run on the lawn and were steadily cropping the coarse grasses and clovers while ignoring the finer lawn grasses. 'They're just like me,' Mike insisted. 'Sooner have simple food than caviar and lobster claws. It's still a bit chilly, isn't it? You can get some really cold days in May.'

'He's hinting,' said Betty, 'that he wants a bread-and-butter pudding for lunch. Oh well – the kids can have the caviar and lobster for their tea.' It was good to find the Tuckers in such good spirits, and when I tried Betty's recipe for bread-and-butter pudding I found it the best I have ever tasted.

Spiced bread-and-butter pudding

8 oz bread (with crusts removed)

2-3 oz butter

2 tablespoons brown sugar

3 oz sultanas, soaked in rum if possible

Grated rind of 1 orange

3 eggs

1 pint creamy milk

1 teaspoon cinnamon

Icing sugar

Spread the bread with softened butter. Mix together the sugar, sultanas, cinnamon and orange rind. Arrange some of the bread, cut into triangles, in a shallow, well greased 2½-pint ovenproof dish. Sprinkle over the sugar mix. Add another layer of buttered bread. Whisk together the eggs and milk and pour over the pudding. Dot with butter. Bake at 180°C (350°F, gas mark 4) for 45-60 minutes until risen and golden. Dust with icing sugar.

June

RECIPES FOR JUNE

Verdant watercress soup

English lamb with asparagus

Salmon and asparagus in pastry

Jean Paul's strawberry tartlets

Strawberry and peppercorn pancakes

Borsetshire 'Heysel' cake

Elizabeth's almond shortbreads

Elderflower champagne

J U N E   N O T E B O O K

Bright blue speedwell, mallow, and St John's wort; red campion, yellow cinquefoil, and wild iris; delicate pink dog roses waving in every hedgerow, and creamy-white cow parsley foaming on every verge! June is the most glorious month for wild flowers. They call cow parsley 'keck' in these parts, but I prefer the old country title 'Queen Anne's lace' because of its fragile, delicate blossom. Walter Gabriel tells me that when he was a lad he used to dig up the parsnip-shaped roots and eat them, and he claims they have a nutty flavour. 'That was eighty years ago, mind,' he said, 'so I could be mistaken.'

The may is fading but the elderflower is in bloom. Pennywort, with its cluster of ivory bells, is growing out of the stonework of the old coachhouse behind Grey Gables.

The big events on the farm are the hay harvest and the sheep-shearing. Brian's shepherd, Sammy Whipple, remembers the amazing 'feast' they used to have for the sheep-shearers when he was young. It would happen on the last day of shearing, and the men would gather in the hot farmhouse kitchen, their clothes thick and smelly from the sheep's wool, and with flies and ticks buzzing and jumping everywhere, and they'd crowd round the table and eat boiled beef and onions. Then they'd eat a plum pudding saved from Christmas! Nowadays Brian just gives his shearing team a few cans of cold beer, and they sit and drink them round the swimming pool.

The smell of new-cut hay is wafted on the warm, gentle breeze, but even that isn't what it was. There used to be over 1,500 kinds of grasses in the traditional, un-chemical-treated hayfields, and many of them contained acids that gave off a multitude of scents when cut and exposed to the sun.

There are only half a dozen varieties of grass in the average hayfield now. Tom says the nearest thing to the smell of an old-fashioned hayfield is the fragrance of meadow-sweet.

In the Grey Gables herb garden, basil and rosemary are in blossom. Basil was once believed to restore failing memory and lighten the heart and mind. All I can promise is that it gives an excellent flavour to tomato dishes. Rosemary is the perfect accompaniment to the new season's lamb, and has long been a token of true love.

Foxes are still keeping their cubs above ground, and you can catch a sight of them playing if you go out in the fields at the right time, and go *quietly* enough. Down by the river a pair of kingfishers are breeding, and Tom tells me that toadlets are starting to leave the pond by Grange Farm. They depart from their nursery a week or two later than froglets, and if they should happen to encounter an adder as they cross Heydon Berrow they will inflate themselves like balloons and stiffen their legs, thus frustrating the adder's attempts to eat them whole.

R E C I P E S F O R J U N E

Incredibly good for you, stuffed to bursting with Vitamin A, Vitamin C, Vitamin E, riboflavin, iron, calcium and phosphorus, watercress is at its best in spring and early summer, and again in the autumn. The Romans thought it was good for the brain; in Ambridge Tony Archer assures me that eating a bunch is a terrific cure for a hangover. 'At least,' he told me, 'that's what my Dad always reckoned, and he was landlord of the pub for years.' An acre of watercress needs a million gallons of pure fresh water *every day* to make it grow, and it should be eaten very soon after purchase. If you need to keep it for any length of time, stand it in a jar of water in a cool place.

There are many recipes for watercress soup, but this is my favourite; the celery, parsley, and salad onions complement the distinctive watercress flavour, and the soup is an attractive, rich, dark-green colour when served at the table.

Verdant watercress soup

Heat butter. Add watercress, parsley, salad onions, celery and seasoning. Cover and cook gently for 10 minutes. Add stock. Re-cover. Simmer for 15 minutes. Liquidise until smooth. Re-heat and thicken if required. Garnish with swirls of cream.

2 oz butter

3 bunches watercress, chopped

1 oz parsley, chopped

1 stick celery, chopped

2 salad onions, chopped

Freshly ground salt and pepper

$1\frac{1}{2}$ pints chicken stock

Cornflour to thicken

A year or two ago I had several lunches at the Mont Blanc restaurant at Little Croxley, and at one memorable meal in early summer we were served what the chef called 'Lamb Argenteuil' – named after the district in France famous for its asparagus. Well, there is no asparagus in the world to beat that from Evesham and the Vale of Am; and there is no lamb as tender and full of flavour as that from the Hassett Hills (the French just can't buy enough of it, to the fury of their own farmers!). There is nothing particularly French about the recipe – it is simply the most delicious lamb casserole imaginable.

English lamb with asparagus

2 lb shoulder meat, cut into 2-3-inch chunks

2 lb fresh asparagus

2 oz butter

4 medium onions

Seasoned flour

$\frac{1}{4}$ pint double cream

Lemon juice

Freshly ground salt and pepper

Wash, scrape and cook the asparagus upright in lightly salted water until tender – 15 to 20 minutes. Drain well and reserve the cooking liquor and the asparagus tips (which should be 3-4 inches long). Liquidise the remaining stems, then sieve to get rid of any stringy bits. You will probably need a little of the cooking liquor to do this.

Trim excess fat from the lamb (as much as possible) and toss in seasoned flour. Brown in a deep frying-pan with melted butter and roughly chopped onions. When brown, gradually stir in about $\frac{1}{2}$-pint of asparagus liquor to make a thickish sauce. Cover the pan and simmer the meat for about an hour, skimming off any fat. When the meat has cooked, and the sauce reduced, add the asparagus purée and the cream. Then add seasoning and lemon juice to taste. Serve with plainly boiled new potatoes and the asparagus tips.

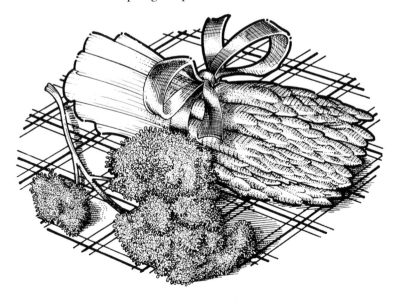

Colonel 'Freddie' Danby is chairman of Ambridge Parish Council and has spent many years of his life serving in the East. 'More often than not my lunch would be a corned beef and chapati sandwich without even a scrape of butter,' he told me. 'I'd sit under the awning of my truck watching the boy boiling up my tea with condensed milk in it, and do you know what I'd dream about? The regimental garden party at Aldershot, with pretty girls, iced punch, and a buffet of cold salmon and asparagus in pastry.'

I agree it is a dish worth dreaming about, and when we have it on the menu at Grey Gables Mr Woolley will often invite the Colonel over for a round of golf, and then suggest, tactfully, 'Why don't you stay for a spot of lunch?'

We serve it as a hot dish, but it is equally delicious when cold. The following will serve six people (or four colonels!).

Salmon and asparagus in pastry

Ask your fishmonger to skin the salmon and bone it into 2 fillets. Mix together the raisins, almonds, ginger and butter, then spread half the mixture on to one of the salmon fillets. Cover this with the other fillet, and spread the rest of the mixture on top. Place the asparagus spears (be sure to cut off any woody bits) on top of that. Season. Cut the pastry in half and roll out 2 rectangles large enough to contain the salmon. Lay the salmon in the centre of one pastry rectangle. Brush the edge of the pastry with egg glaze. Place the other pastry piece on top and press the pastry edges together. Make three slashes in the pastry so that steam can escape. Decorate the top with bits of fish-shaped pastry and brush with the rest of the egg glaze. Bake in a pre-heated oven at 220°C (425°F, gas mark 7) for about 30 minutes, until golden brown. Garnish with chopped parsley.

If eaten hot a delightful accompaniment is herb sauce (see over).

Ingredients
2½ lb salmon (tailpiece will do)
4 oz butter
3 pieces preserved ginger, chopped
2 tablespoons raisins
2 tablespoons blanched almonds, chopped
12 asparagus spears
Freshly ground salt and pepper
1 lb shortcrust pastry (see page 57)
Beaten egg for glaze
Parsley for garnish

Herb sauce

2 oz butter
2 shallots, peeled and chopped
1 tablespoon chopped parsley
2 tablespoons chopped chervil
2 teaspoons chopped tarragon
1 teaspoon flour
½ pint single cream
Freshly ground salt and pepper
1 teaspoon Dijon mustard
2 egg yolks
Lemon juice

Melt the butter in a frying pan. Add shallots and herbs and cook over low heat until soft. Stir in the flour. Keep back 1 tablespoon of cream but add the rest. Season. Simmer, stirring all the time, for 10 minutes. Beat in the mustard. Mix the remaining cream with the egg yolks and beat into the sauce. Stir until it thickens slightly (but don't let it boil!). Add lemon juice to taste.

'June, *flaming* June,' Higgs will keep grumbling, as he sweats his way along the rows of strawberries in the kitchen garden, gathering up the fruit in Trudy Porter's wicker basket and checking that each plant is surrounded by straw as a protection against dirt and slugs. When I have friends round to tea I pick the strawberries myself, choosing those that are small and full of flavour, and I gather them in the afternoon because strawberries should be eaten warm from the sun. I like them with the merest sprinkling of caster sugar and a dollop of thick yellow clotted cream. At Brookfield they eat them with cream straight from the dairy, which is even better. I called by and found them all sitting out in the orchard, eating the first strawberries of the season with thin slices of brown bread-and-butter.

Tea on the terrace at Grey Gables would not be complete without one of Jean Paul's strawberry tartlets. Fresh strawberries glistening with a redcurrant glaze, the creamy cool vanilla taste of confectioners' custard, and the crisp sweetness of a good shortcrust pastry. Could there be a more perfect combination? Well, Jean Paul's secret is to add a dash of Cointreau to the confectioners' custard, and that, he says, is what makes his tartlets so famous.

Jean Paul's strawberry tartlets

Make the pastry cases (for Jean Paul's method with pastry see page 57) and cook in a pre-heated oven at 200°C (400°F, gas mark 6) for 20-25 minutes. They should be a pale golden brown. Set on one side to cool. To make the custard, heat the milk with the vanilla pod to boiling point, then take off the heat and allow to infuse. Whisk the caster sugar into the egg yolks and beat until it is like thick cream. Add the plain flour and the cornflour. Pour the milk (minus the vanilla pod!) over the mix and stir energetically. Pour into the pan and heat gently, stirring until the mixture thickens. When it has, add a few drops of Cointreau. Pour the custard into the tartlet cases. When cool, cover with strawberries and brush with a glaze made from redcurrant jelly.

Pastry

8 oz self-raising flour

5 oz butter

1 tablespoon soft brown sugar

1 medium egg, beaten

Filling

$\frac{3}{4}$ pint milk

Vanilla pod

4 oz caster sugar

5 egg yolks

2 tablespoons plain flour

1 tablespoon cornflour

Cointreau

8 oz strawberries

Redcurrant jelly for glaze

There are those who would regard it as a great vulgarity to flambé perfectly good strawberries in a sickly sauce of sugar, crushed green peppercorns and liqueur. Mr Woolley, however, is not among them. This is his favourite summer dessert.

Strawberry and peppercorn pancakes

4 pancakes
1 teaspoon drained green Madagascar peppercorns
2 oz butter
2 oz sugar
2 tablespoons Grand Marnier
8 oz strawberries

Crush half the peppercorns, using a mortar and pestle or the flat side of a heavy knife. Melt the butter in a frying pan. Add the sugar and crushed peppercorns. Keep the heat low until the sugar has dissolved. Increase the heat and cook rapidly until the mixture is brown. While that is happening warm the Grand Marnier. Stir it into the butter/sugar mixture and set it alight. The moment the flames subside add the strawberries. Toss them about, over heat, for half a minute. Add the remaining whole peppercorns. Spoon the hot strawberries into pancakes, sprinkle with caster sugar, and serve immediately with chilled pouring cream.

'Chariots of gold,' says Timothy;
'Silvery wings,' says Elaine;
'A bumpity ride in a wagon of hay
For me,' says Jane.

Alas for Walter de la Mare's Jane, the wagons of loose hay are no longer with us. Neither are the rows of men scything their way across the sweet-smelling meadows, nor the wonderful hayfield teas of yore! At one time whole families would spend the day out in the fields, mowing and turning the hay and loading it high on the wain. 'I was the gamekeeper's son, but we all had to turn out for haymaking and corn harvest,' Tom told me. 'It was hard work and my poor skin would be tortured by hayseeds and insect bites – but we did get good food brought to us! Bread, cheese, ham, and huge wedges of fruit cake to give us energy. Nobody ever drank cider during the day but only cold tea, which is a very refreshing drink.'

Everything is mechanised now, and haymaking is a two-man job at most, with both of them sitting on tractors. But at Home Farm, Jennifer loves to take little Kate out to the hayfield for a good old-fashioned picnic, and she often makes this Borsetshire 'Heysel' cake. It's moist and filling, and if you are very wicked you might eat it hot from the oven, with butter on it.

Borsetshire 'Heysel' cake

Melt the butter in a large saucepan. Add the sugar, the sultanas, raisins and currants, and the glacé cherries. Add a generous shake of mixed spice. Add the milk. Bring to the boil and simmer for five minutes. Take off the heat and allow to cool (otherwise you will cook the egg you have to add next!) Add the bicarbonate of soda, the beaten egg and the flour. Make sure the flour is properly folded in. Pour the mixture into a cake tin, and cook for 45 minutes at 165°C (300°F, gas mark 2). Test with a skewer, and cook for another 5 or 10 minutes if necessary.

4 oz butter
4 oz sugar
1 cup sultanas/raisins/currants (mix as you wish)
Mixed spice
4 oz glacé cherries (or more if you like them)
$\frac{1}{2}$ pint milk
$\frac{1}{2}$ teaspoon bicarbonate of soda
1 beaten egg
8 oz self-raising flour

Whenever Elizabeth Archer wants something from her father she makes a batch of these almond shortbreads, and gives them to him to eat with his morning coffee and afternoon tea. 'They're so good,' she says, 'he just looks at me, glows with pride, and mutters about the money spent on my education not having been wasted after all.' She says the recipe is one of four she learned during Home Economics at her boarding school. She has forgotten the other three.

Elizabeth's almond shortbreads

4 oz butter
2 oz sugar
2 oz ground almonds
1 oz ground semolina
4 oz plain flour

Cream together the butter and sugar until fluffy and light. Gradually mix in the flour, ground almonds and semolina. Work into a dough with your fingers. Chill in the fridge for about half an hour. Press into a buttered 7-inch shallow round tin, mark into sections and prick with a fork. Cook at 180°C (350°F, gas mark 4) for 20 to 30 minutes. It should be the colour of ripe corn – be careful not to overcook! For easy removal, use a tin with a separate base.

Summer is not truly come (so they say) until the elder is in flower, and it ends only when the elderberries are ripe. The heavy-scented blossoms, creamy among the dark leaves, appear in late May or early June depending on where you live, and they can be used to make a sparkling, thirst-quenching summer drink. It was Pru Forrest who gave me the recipe, and she got it from Mary Pound who used to live at Ambridge Farm with her husband Ken.

Elderflower champagne

2 heads elderflower (picked when they are just out)
1 lemon
1½ lb white sugar
2 tablespoons white wine vinegar
1 gallon cold water

Pick the heads when the blossom has newly opened. Take off the green stems, if there are any, and put the heads into a bowl. Sprinkle with juice from the lemon. Grate the rind, and add together with the vinegar and sugar. Add the cold water. Leave for 24 hours. Strain into bottles. Cork firmly. Lay the bottles on their sides. Within two weeks the 'champagne' should be sparkling and ready to drink. Unopened bottles will keep for up to 3 months.

July

R E C I P E S   F O R   J U L Y

Chilled plum soup

Sugar peas with bacon and chicken livers

French bean salad

Churcham stuffed loin of veal

Crispy roast duck with orange sauce

Trudy Porter's cherry batter pudding

Cherry and hazelnut crumble

Raspberry pavlova cake

J U L Y   N O T E B O O K

Now comes full summer, a time of deeper colours and stronger scents. Scarlet poppies and mustard-coloured charlock jostle by the farm track, driven out of the cornfield by modern chemical sprays but sprouting up on every bit of untreated land they can find. Each poppy contains 30,000 seeds – a challenge to the most ruthless and efficient of farmers!

In the deep woodland shade are purple and white foxgloves, containing the poison digitalin; out in the sun ox-eyed daisies, campion, and campanula. Along the Am is a pink swathe of rosebay willow herb, another plant that thrives on any scrap of land it can find. Fifty years ago it was quite uncommon, and it was only during the war that it began to spread, often on bomb sites. A visitor to Grey Gables tells me that in America they call it 'fireweed' because it is the first plant to seed itself on land devastated by forest fires.

In the hedgerows are white trumpets of woodbine, and on the roadside verges the lovely violet-blue flowers of the meadow cranesbill. Then, of course, there is the twining, sweet-scented honeysuckle. Its bugles are filled with a nectar of sucrose, fructose and glucose that drives the humble (and I dare say bumble) bees mad with desire. But they cannot reach it. The honeysuckle guards her sweetness until twilight when night-flying hawkmoths are abroad. Then her corollas become more fragrant than ever, inviting the hawk moths to penetrate them with their elongated tongues.

'It's the story of life itself,' a farmer friend of mine once said, after we had watched a bee desperately trying to bore its way into a tube of nectar that swayed and tossed in the July breeze.

Two families of birds are nesting in the old coachhouse. A pair of blackbirds have settled themselves on a shelf, and made a nest that shapes itself round the end of a petrol can; and a pair of swallows have built their little mud abode on the dynamo light of Higgs's bicycle. Each morning I sit in the yard, drinking my coffee in the sunshine, and watching the birds fly in and out with food. The swallows' nestlings are quiet, but the blackbird chicks set up a frenzied noise whenever they think worms are approaching. Higgs dislikes little birds, and grumbles constantly because I won't allow him to use either the petrol can or his bicycle. The swallows seem to know him as an enemy. Swooping with terrifying speed into the dark entrance to the coachhouse they nearly made him fall over as he came out after searching for a garden rake. He wants to know who will clean up the mess of droppings under their mud nest, and is also demanding compensation for acid rot to his chrome bicycle light.

Down by Arkwright Lake, after a sudden July storm, Tom pokes around in the heronry with a stick, prodding at the pellets of undigested food left under the nests. He says he is looking to see how much fur is inside them, because although herons normally eat fish they are not averse to a nice fat mole. 'Not that they often get the chance,' says Tom, 'but moles are sometimes driven to the surface if their runs are flooded by a thunderstorm. That's when the herons swoop down and gobble them up.'

He prods open a pellet, to reveal a little bundle of lovely bluey-velvet fur . . .

RECIPES FOR JULY

A summer dinner party at Home Farm. Jennifer is cool and relaxed (although only ten of us, the wonderful Penelope from Penny Hassett has been brought in to do the food) and Brian is wearing a new and extremely well-cut dinner jacket. We drink Pimms by the pool, and Tony says he'd really rather have a can of beer if nobody minds, and Brian says, 'No problem, old chap,' and admires Tony's made-up plush velvet bow-tie. 'It's on elastic,' Tony explains. 'Saves having to mess about tying a knot.' 'Wonderful,' says Brian, 'does it light up and twirl round and round as well?'

Jennifer kicks him, and we go inside to eat. Although Penelope's saddle of lamb is divine, and the chestnut and strawberry roulade is delicious ('Actually, I made it myself!' says Jennifer, anxiously), it is the chilled plum soup that wins most admiration. Penelope has been providing enterprising cuisine in people's homes ever since she graduated from the Birmingham College of Food in 1985, and she says this summer starter is a great favourite. In winter it can be made using canned plums.

Chilled plum soup

In a pan combine plums, water, wine, sugar, lemon juice and spices. Simmer gently until tender, then sieve. Blend the cornflour with a little water, add to the fruit and bring to the boil. Simmer gently until the soup thickens, stirring all the time. Leave to chill and stir in the buttermilk.

(serves 6 people)

3 lb English plums

$\frac{1}{2}$ pint water

$\frac{1}{2}$ pint red wine

8 oz demerara sugar

2 tablespoons lemon juice

$\frac{1}{2}$ teaspoon mixed spice

Pinch of ground cloves

1 tablespoon cornflour

$\frac{1}{2}$ pint buttermilk

When Shula married Mark she was given a wok for a wedding present, and made the momentous discovery (among the many momentous discoveries of married life) that wok-cooked sugar peas are crisp, juicy, and utterly delicious! Many people still regard sugar peas with suspicion, however, clearly regarding the eating of peapods as a degenerate and unwholesome activity particularly when they have a foreign name like *mangetout*. Sugar peas, though, have been grown in England for centuries, and there's even a recipe for them in a 17th-century cookery book. In Borsetshire they were traditionally served with 'Borsetshire Duck' – a shoulder of Hassett lamb trussed in the shape of a duck and served swimming in a dark-green sugar pea lake – or as an accompaniment to Guard of Honour. You can buy imported *mangetout* very early in the season, and Mr Woolley always wants me to put them on the menu in March or early April to impress diners who crave for something different. I firmly resist his pressure, for like baby new potatoes, sugar peas ought to be eaten within hours of harvesting, and ought not to be flown about the earth in smelly aeroplanes before reaching the table. In late June and July they are perfect, and when you tire of eating them on their own (lightly steamed or briefly plunged into fast moving boiling water) you will be delighted by Shula's wonderful first course. And it does not, incidentally, even need a wok!

Sugar peas with bacon and chicken livers

1 lb sugar peas (or *mangetout*)
3 tablespoons olive oil
2 tablespoons white wine vinegar with tarragon
4 oz chicken livers
2 rashers smoked back bacon, cut into strips
16-24 small bread cubes
Freshly ground black pepper as required

Cook the sugar peas for a few minutes in boiling water. Take out while still crisp, drain, and toss with the oil and vinegar in a warm dish. Chop and season the chicken livers. Cook the bacon strips in their own fat until crisp. Remove and keep hot. Fry the bread in the bacon fat, adding more oil if necessary. Add the croutons to the bacon. Quickly fry the chicken livers in the remaining fat, but remove them while still pink in the middle. Drain any excess dressing from the sugar peas, and mix in the hot bacon, croutons, and chicken livers. Serve at once.

This can either be a starter for four, or a delicious light lunch for two!

Apart from sugar peas, July brings a sudden abundance of many delicious vegetables. Green Windsor broad beans are George's favourite – I sometimes think he grows nothing else in the garden at The Stables – and I love courgettes, particularly when they been chopped into thick rounds and pan-fried with mixed herbs until crisp and brown on the outside. Later in the month comes the maincrop of French beans, called 'snap beans' in many parts because they snap cleanly when you break them. When the first tiny, tender green beans appear they need nothing more than a quick look at a pan of boiling water, a rapid pass under a salt and pepper mill, and a knob of butter! But as the maincrop comes in you might like to try this dish, which was served with cold chicken at the Ambridge WI garden meeting last summer. The beans, eggs, and dressing do make a perfect combination.

French bean salad

Top and tail the beans and cook in boiling water for about 5 minutes. Drain and rinse under cold running water. Boil the eggs for 10 minutes. After cooling in cold water, shell them and cut them into quarters. Squeeze the lemon, skin and crush the garlic, then mix the lemon juice, garlic, and olive oil vigorously. Season. Put the French beans into a dish with the hardboiled egg quarters on top. Sprinkle finely chopped spring onions over them. Finally, pour on the lemon and oil dressing.

1 lb young French beans

4 eggs

Juice of a lemon

1 clove garlic

2 tablespoons olive oil

Freshly ground salt and pepper

6 spring onions, finely chopped

If you see Dutch veal for sale it will probably be a pale anaemic colour. English veal, on the other hand, will be a delicate salmon pink. There is a very good reason for this, according to my friend Richard who raises veal on a smallholding near Churcham. The Dutch, he says, keep their calves cruelly penned in crates, in semi-darkness, and forcefeed them. In England most farmers let the calves roam free in groups of between ten and twenty, in strawfilled pens where they can feed at will. As a result English calves grow according to nature, and their meat has a healthy look to it. That's what my friend says, anyway! His wife Susan cooks loin of veal with a wonderful bacon stuffing.

Churcham stuffed loin of veal

4 lb loin of veal, boned
1 medium onion
4 rashers streaky bacon
3 oz suet
4 oz breadcrumbs
1 tablespoon chopped parsley
1 teaspoon grated lemon rind
Knob of butter
Freshly ground salt and pepper
A little flour
Glass of dry white wine (optional)

Ask your butcher to bone the veal, and use the bones to make a gravy stock. To make the stuffing: finely chop the onion and cook in butter until transparent. Remove from the pan, turn up the heat, and crisp the bacon rashers. Add these to the onion, and mix in the suet and breadcrumbs. Add the chopped parsley and grated lemon rind and seasoning. Spread the mixture on the veal, then roll it up and tie it firmly with string. Prick the fatty top of the joint, and season with freshly ground salt and pepper. Cook for 40 minutes per pound and 40 minutes over at 180°C (350°F, gas mark 4). Baste during cooking. When the joint is cooked, make a gravy by adding a little flour to the pan juices and mixing in some of the bone stock and a glass of dry white wine if you wish.

Freddie Danby will talk for hours about ducks. Khaki Campbells are boring birds but they do lay lots of eggs (and that means lots of super omelettes). Aylesbury ducks are the most stupid birds imaginable, but they grow big, meaty breasts after only ten or twelve weeks. Muscovy ducks? Well Muscovy ducks are supremely intelligent. 'And they're very good-looking,' I remember him once saying, as Jemima and Rebecca came waddling round the side of Ambridge Hall and pecked at the kitchen door demanding food. Outside, perched on a rickety fence and swaying in the wind, Mr Drake watched the world with a beady eye, and Freddie Danby turned his back before

saying in a low voice: 'And of course Muscovies do have the most wonderful *flavour* of any duck imaginable!'

Few of us get the chance to taste roast Muscovy duck, but we can all avoid those fatty, greasy, and sadly disappointing roast ducklings that are served with sickly black-cherry sauce in many restaurants that ought to know better.

Duck should be cooked until the fat has drained away from the carcase and the skin is crisp and sweet, and this is how to do it.

Crispy roast duck with orange sauce

1 duck or duckling
Melted honey
6 oranges
1 glass red wine
$\frac{1}{2}$ glass medium dry sherry
2 tablespoons redcurrant jelly
1 heaped tablespoon cornflour
1 onion
Freshly ground salt and pepper
Watercress for garnish

Make sure the duck is dry. Prick the skin all over and sprinkle with freshly ground salt and pepper. Pop a raw onion inside the duck. Cook for 30 minutes per pound at 180°C (350°F, gas mark 4) on a wire rack, turning once. Prick the skin again during cooking to allow the fat to drain away. Ten minutes before the end of cooking, or when the fat has pretty well stopped dripping from the bird, brush the skin with melted honey. Turn up the heat to crisp the skin, but watch carefully that it does not burn. In a saucepan mix the coarsely grated peel and juice of four oranges (thin-skinned ones are best) with the red wine, sherry and redcurrant jelly. Stir in the cornflour thoroughly, then bring to the boil and simmer for a few minutes. By this time it will have thickened to a delicious aromatic sauce. Garnish the duck with watercress and the other two oranges cut into slices.

English cherries come into the shops in July, and I find them quite irresistible. I buy half a pound in Borchester and sit in the riverside gardens enjoying the sunshine, and then I 'test' a cherry for sweetness and juiciness, and a moment later I find all I've got is a brown paper bag full of cherry stones. If I *do* manage to get any cherries back to Grey Gables, however, I stone them, soak them in liqueur (I prefer Cointreau to Kirsch, but it's all a matter of taste) and eat them with home-made vanilla ice-cream. Here, though, are two hot cherry puddings. Trudy Porter makes cherry batter pudding for the staff dining room, where Tom Forrest votes it an all-time favourite, and the cherry and hazelnut crumble is a famous pudding at our Sunday Lunches.

Trudy Porter's cherry batter pudding

1 lb sweet black English cherries
4 oz caster sugar
8 oz plain flour
Pinch salt
4 eggs, separated
$\frac{1}{2}$ pint milk

Butter a $2\frac{1}{2}$-pint pudding basin and put the stoned cherries in the bottom. Sprinkle 2 oz sugar on the cherries. Separate the eggs and beat the yolks into the flour and salt in a bowl. Gradually whisk in the milk as you would with pancake batter. Beat the 4 egg whites until they are stiff and dry, then fold into the batter mixture. Pour this over the cherries. Cover and steam for an hour. When ready to serve, turn out on a hot plate and sprinkle with the remaining sugar. Serve with single cream.

Cherry and hazelnut crumble

Stone the cherries and put them in a shallow dish with the caster sugar. Cook them in the oven at 170°C (325°F, gas mark 3) until the juice runs. Using a slotted spoon, put the cherries in a clean buttered dish, leaving most of the juice behind. To make the crumble topping rub the butter into the flour until it resembles breadcrumbs. Stir in the soft brown sugar and nuts. Sprinkle the crumble mix on the cherries and cook until the top just turns a honey colour – about 20 minutes at 170°C (325°F, gas mark 3). Serve with single cream.

2 lb cherries
4 oz caster sugar
8 oz plain flour
4 oz butter
4 oz soft brown sugar
4 oz chopped hazelnuts (or mixed chopped nuts if preferred)

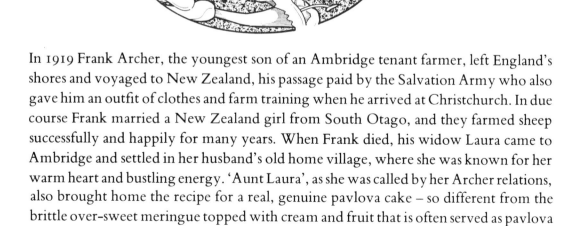

In 1919 Frank Archer, the youngest son of an Ambridge tenant farmer, left England's shores and voyaged to New Zealand, his passage paid by the Salvation Army who also gave him an outfit of clothes and farm training when he arrived at Christchurch. In due course Frank married a New Zealand girl from South Otago, and they farmed sheep successfully and happily for many years. When Frank died, his widow Laura came to Ambridge and settled in her husband's old home village, where she was known for her warm heart and bustling energy. 'Aunt Laura', as she was called by her Archer relations, also brought home the recipe for a real, genuine pavlova cake – so different from the brittle over-sweet meringue topped with cream and fruit that is often served as pavlova in Britain.

In Australia and New Zealand they have many tropical fruits to choose from, but, although we can get kiwi fruit and pineapple without difficulty, I prefer it with bananas and English raspberries – and raspberries in July are at their very best.

Raspberry pavlova cake

6 egg whites

Pinch of salt

8 oz caster sugar

4 oz ground almonds

1 teaspoon vanilla essence

1 teaspoon wine vinegar

1 dessertspoon cornflour

$\frac{1}{2}$ pint whipped cream

4 bananas

$\frac{1}{2}$ lb raspberries

Beat egg whites and a pinch of salt until very stiff. Add 4 oz caster sugar, a teaspoonful at a time, and keep beating until the mixture is thick and glossy (this is easy with an electric mixer). Continue beating slowly (electric mixer on slowest speed) and add another 4 oz sugar and 4 oz ground almonds together with the vanilla essence, wine vinegar and cornflour. Turn the mixture out on a baking tray covered with greaseproof paper. Bake at 150°C (300°F, gas mark 2) but do not allow to go brown. After about 45 minutes it should have developed a firm shell on the outside, but this is not the kind of meringue that dries hard. When ready, turn the meringue upside down on a serving dish so the marshmallowy surface is upwards. Cover this with sliced bananas, then with whipped cream. Cover completely with fresh raspberries.

August

RECIPES FOR AUGUST

Tomato, egg and anchovy salad

Green beans with parmesan and thyme

Pork fillet in pastry with mushroom sauce

Apple and pork-liver pâté

'The Brookfield Barbecue'

Old-fashioned lemon curdcake

Kathy Holland's freezer jam

Borbury fruited tea scones

AUGUST NOTEBOOK

Poor, sad August! Her withered hedgerows full of the dying glories of June and July; the green leaves of summer turning dull and dusty; all that glorious, foaming cow parsley reduced to gaunt dry stems and blackened seedpods. Even the air is full of thunderbugs and insects from the cornfields. No wonder this is seen as the month to make tracks for the seaside or (even better) for Scotland.

Red corn poppies are still bursting into bloom, of course, and creamy yarrow, which is said to be a herb of power and divination strong against enemies! In the undergrowth you can spy out blue-flowering hedge woundwort, and red dead-nettle which was once used by cottagers as a pot herb and as pig swill. And there is a promise of things to come. The bramble is in flower in the hedgerows, and pheasants stalk the fields with impunity – reminding me of blackberry jelly and a rather good recipe for pheasant casserole!

It is in cottage gardens that August flowers are at their best, and Shula and Mark have done wonders at Glebe Cottage. There are pink and white hollyhocks, a mass of blue petunias, sweet peas climbing round the water barrel, and sweet-scented tobacco plants and stocks along the paths. In the spring Mark bought Shula a rose bush called Schoolgirl ('Which is how I'll always think of you,' he is reported to have said, rather oddly, because he never knew her as a schoolgirl) and its delicate apricot flowers are now in bloom.

The big village event is the Flower and Produce Show. In the morning everybody rushes down to the hall with their entries of cakes, jams, chutneys, vegetables and flowers. Then, at two-thirty, everybody rushes back to see what the judges have decided. Pat Archer still talks bitterly about the year she dusted her Victoria Sponge with icing sugar (which is against the rules) and was disqualified. 'Sixteen people watched me do it,' she claims, 'and not one of them said a word!' Joe Grundy goes on and on about the 'shilling teas' they used to serve in the old days. 'As much bread-and-butter and cake as you could eat for a bob,' he grumbles, when Martha makes him pay twenty pence for tea and biscuits.

In the August cornfields huge combines are at work, and when the weather threatens to break you can see them late at night, their huge lights moving slowly up and down as they harvest the oats, barley, and finally the wheat.

Honeybees are about, and you must be patient if one lands on your head. It will bring you good luck and make you rich.

After the corn is cut foxes take their cubs to kale or other root crops, and remain above ground as a family group unless disturbed by the hunt. Cub-hunting starts late in the month, and is designed to teach hounds – who have been strictly taught *not* to chase cats, dogs, and sheep – that they can and must chase foxes.

In the August afternoon grasshoppers play their mating game by rubbing their back legs together, and in the evening swifts can be seen in companies, climbing high into the sunset, where they will sleep sliding through the cool air. Badger cubs come out at dusk, and quarter the pasture for worms who leave their tunnels to mate on the wet grass. The badgers chomp them up while they're courting, as do foxes, hedgehogs and shrews. Worms have a very tense sex life.

RECIPES FOR AUGUST

Tomatoes are ripening, and the entire village, or so it seems, begins to argue fiercely about which variety is the best to grow. Walter Gabriel has tomatoes in pots in his living-room window, and favours a modern variety called Tiny Tim (they remind him, he says, of a baby elephant of that name which he once possessed) while Jethro Larkin grows Moneymaker in the glass lean-to at Woodbine Cottage. Walter says that Moneymaker lack flavour, Jethro disagrees and Mr Fletcher, from Glebelands, invities them both to look at his Eurocross F1 hybrids.

On a hot, dusty August day it is hard to beat a simple tomato salad, dressed with olive oil and sprinkled with chopped spring onion and parsley. After a week or two of the season, though, even the most flavoursome tomato gets a little boring just by itself. I never tire of the following recipe. Served with crusty French bread and a glass of cool English wine, it is my favourite lunchtime dish, and it makes a delicious first course for a dinner party. It will even improve by keeping for 24 hours, so that the tomato juices and salty anchovy flavour can soak into the eggs.

Tomato, egg and anchovy salad

Slice the hardboiled eggs and place in a layer on the bottom of the dish. Place the drained and dried anchovy fillets in a criss-cross pattern across them. Sprinkle on the capers and gherkins. Scald and skin the tomatoes, and cut them in half. Place them, cut side down, over the egg and anchovy mix so that they cover the entire dish. Make a dressing from the oil, vinegar, mustard, and freshly ground salt and pepper. Add the tomato purée and blend in well. Pour the dressing over the tomatoes. Sprinkle with freshly chopped parsley.

8 firm medium tomatoes
6 hardboiled eggs
1 tin anchovy fillets
1 tablespoon capers
2 gherkins, sliced
6 tablespoons olive oil
2 tablespoons wine vinegar
1 teaspoon mustard powder
2 tablespoons tomato purée
Fresh parsley for garnish

Runner beans are everywhere in the cottage gardens. Susan Carter has them twining up a trellis, Detective-Sergeant Barry has a double row of them in an otherwise deserted vegetable plot, and at Glebelands they riot round wigwams made out of long canes. Walter Gabriel doesn't believe in using expensive canes, though. He cuts his bean poles from the withy trees down by the Am, and keeps them, year after year, until they warp, become brittle with age, and finally snap. 'The same would have happened to me,' he chuckles, 'if I didn't refresh myself with a glass of my Special now and then!'

Scarlet Emperor is a favourite variety, and it is considered acceptable to attach little weights to your show entries, so that they will grow straight and long. The bright red flowers are a delight to look at, and the beans look splendid when laid out in the vegetable tent at the Flower Show . . . but why are they so *boring* to eat?

True, they do have a succulent, very beany flavour when cooked young, and I always associate them for some reason with lamb chops and boiled potatoes, the standard Saturday stand-by lunch at home when I was little.

But they soon become coarse, stringy, and flavourless. In every garden you see them hanging, unwanted, from beanpole and trellis; at night people creep round leaving bundles of them on friends' doorsteps.

Here, though, is a recipe to save the runner bean. We serve it regularly at Grey Gables in the summer, as an accompaniment to roast meat. Poor runner bean though – I have to admit the recipe is even nicer with French beans, and out of this world with sugar peas!

Green beans with parmesan and thyme

1 lb green beans
2 oz butter
1 tablespoon olive oil
2 tablespoons thyme leaves, stripped from the stems
2 cloves garlic, crushed
2 heaped tablespoons grated parmesan cheese
Freshly ground pepper
Pinch of salt

Prepare the beans and cut into 2-inch pieces. Cook for 5 minutes in boiling, salted water. Drain and keep warm. In a pan mix together the butter, olive oil, thyme leaves, and crushed garlic. Heat gently for 5 minutes. Stir in the beans, season with black pepper, and keep heating for a minute or two. Just before the beans are to be served stir in the parmesan cheese.

August brings field mushrooms, fragrant and delicious, and Tom Forrest is the man who knows where to find them. In the early hours of dawn he trots out, paper bag in hand, and makes his way to a likely corner of Brookfield pasture, or a stubble-field at Home Farm that was full of waving corn only a day or two before. Sometimes, while out exercising my horse Ivor, I find him muttering sorrowfully over bits of mushroom that have been snuffled over and squashed by a grazing cow. 'They don't *like* mushrooms, so why don't they leave 'em alone?' he complains.

But he rarely goes home without enough to eat for breakfast, and the wonderful aroma of fried bacon and mushrooms is soon wafting out from his kitchen window.

August also brings a good supply of Grenadier cooking apples, and the following recipe includes a sauce made from fresh field mushrooms (the other sort will *do*, of course) and a pork-liver pâté stuffing made with apple. It is delicious eaten hot, but also makes a tasty cold lunch on a summer's day.

Pork fillet in pastry with mushroom sauce

Cut the fillet in half lengthways and spread one half with the pâté. Sprinkle with chopped sage and place the other half on top to form a sandwich. (You can, of course, use two whole fillets and double up all the ingredients). Wrap the rashers of bacon round the fillet and secure with cocktail sticks. Season. Heat the oil in a frying pan and brown the fillet all over. Remove from the pan and allow to cool. Grate margarine, add the flour, and make pastry in usual way. Roll it out into a thin rectangle and make a parcel by wrapping the pork fillet in it. Place the parcel, with the join underneath, on a greased baking tray. Decorate with left-over pastry and glaze with beaten egg. Cook in a preheated oven at 220°C (425°C, gas mark 7) for a quarter of an hour. Reduce to 180°C (350°F, gas mark 4) and continue cooking for 25 minutes.

Pastry
8 oz plain flour
6 oz hard margarine, chilled
Pinch of salt
Cold water to mix
Filling
1 pork fillet (about 12 oz)
2–3 oz apple and pork-liver pâté (see over)
6 rashers streaky bacon, derinded
3 or 4 sage leaves, finely chopped
1 tablespoon oil
Freshly ground salt and pepper
Beaten egg for glaze

Mushroom sauce

1 oz butter

4 oz mushrooms, chopped

1½ tablespoons plain flour

Pinch of ground nutmeg

¼ pint water

Few drops Worcestershire sauce

1 dessertspoon mushroom ketchup

Freshly ground salt and pepper

Melt the butter and fry the mushrooms for a few minutes. Add the flour and cook, stirring, for a minute. Add the Worcestershire sauce and mushroom ketchup to the water and gradually stir in. Bring to the boil, stirring, and simmer for a few minutes. Season to taste and add the nutmeg. Serve hot.

Apple and pork-liver pâté

2 oz onions, roughly chopped

5 oz Grenadier apples (or Bramleys if available), peeled cored and chopped

¾ lb pig's liver with the tough sinew removed

6 oz streaky bacon, derinded

4 fl oz red wine

1 tablespoon water

1 teaspoon fresh thyme leaves (or a pinch or two of dried thyme)

Freshly ground salt and pepper

A little butter

Coarsely mince (or finely chop) the onion, apple, liver and bacon. Put the mixture into a saucepan with the wine, water, thyme and seasoning. Cover pan, bring to the boil, then gently simmer for 30 minutes, stirring from time to time. Allow to cool a little. Place in an electric blender, and blend until smooth.

The pâté which is not required to stuff the fillet of pork should be put in a china dish and covered with melted butter. (Remember, after melting the butter, to let it stand and skim off any salt sediment before pouring over the pâté.)

Once a year, generally at the end of July or the beginning of August (depending on the start of the corn harvest), a remarkable event takes place at Brookfield Farm – the menfolk do the cooking!

They don't go in for anything very elaborate, mind you. Phil will not be discovered slaving over *Saint-Pierre Fleurs de Courge* or David agonising over *Marjolaine de foie gras*. But it is enough of an occasion to bring all the Archer family together on a Saturday evening. Nobody (Elizabeth assures me, with only a hint of sarcasm) would dream of missing the Brookfield Barbecue.

If you look closely at the actual work you find that Phil and David are not *quite* the only people involved. Jill is responsible for the salads (red bean and pepper; iceberg lettuce with avocado and kiwi fruit; apple, celery, and mushroom in mayonnaise) and Shula makes the old-fashioned pastry-crust curdcake. Elizabeth buys the bread rolls and warms them in the oven, and yet another female (me!) supplies three of the marinades for the meat.

But it is undoubtedly Phil who stands over the barbecue when the time comes, turning the skewers and tossing sprigs of rosemary and curls of orange peel onto the flames. And David makes a great fuss over his sauce for the spare ribs, a potent mixture of dark-brown sugar, soy sauce, wine vinegar, mustard and tomato purée. 'It's an age-old secret recipe handed down to the youngest son at Brookfield for six generations, ever since great-great grandad Archer came back from the Spanish Main,' he says, and Jill says, 'What he means is he got it off the back of a recipe card in Tesco's.'

Here are my own marinade recipes.

Pork kebabs with courgettes

Lean pork cubes cut from leg or shoulder meat ($1\frac{1}{2}$ lb)

1 small courgette per person

Marinade

6 tablespoons soy sauce (rich variety)

6 tablespoons pineapple juice

3 teaspoons finely chopped root ginger

2 cloves garlic, crushed

1 teaspoon mustard powder

2 tablespoons dry sherry

2 tablespoons water

1 tablespoon olive oil

Mix the marinade ingredients and place the pork cubes in it for 24 hours. When ready to cook, alternate pork cubes and slices of courgette on skewers. While on the barbecue brush with marinade from time to time.

Lamb kebabs with yoghurt

Lean leg of lamb cut into cubes ($1\frac{1}{2}$ lb)

Firm tomatoes

Onions

Marinade

5 oz plain yoghurt (the live variety if possible)

1 lemon

2 teaspoons salt

1 teaspoon black pepper

1 small onion

Grate the small onion and mix with the yoghurt, the juice of the lemon, and the salt and pepper. Place the meat cubes in this marinade for at least 24 hours. Skewer alternately with tomato halves and chunks of onion, and brush with the marinade while on the barbecue.

Lamb kebabs with herbs

Lean leg of lamb cut into cubes ($1\frac{1}{2}$ lb)

Green peppers

Firm tomatoes

Mushrooms

Marinade

4 tablespoons olive oil

Juice of a lemon

1 large bay leaf, crumbled

2 cloves garlic, crushed

1 tablespoon finely chopped rosemary

Freshly ground salt and pepper

Mix the marinade and place the meat cubes in it for at least 4 hours. Skewer alternately with the peppers, tomatoes, and mushrooms. Brush the marinade over the meat during cooking.

Cheesecakes made with a base of crushed digestive biscuits are very popular these days, and very nice they are too. But I prefer this old-fashioned lemon curdcake with a shortcrust pastry case, and it was a great success when Shula served it with thick cream at the Brookfield Barbecue.

Old-fashioned lemon curdcake

Make pastry in the usual way and line a 7-inch flan dish or tin. Preheat the oven to 180°C (350°F, gas mark 4) and bake for 15 minutes, preferably on a baking tray. Remove from the oven and turn oven down to 170°C (325°F, gas mark 3). For the filling, beat together the cheese, sugar, eggs, lemon juice and rind. As the mixture is rather stiff an electric mixer is useful. Stir the cornflour into the cream and add this to the mixture. Pour the filling into the partly cooked pastry case. Sprinkle the raisins over the top of the filling. Bake for half an hour and allow to get cold before eating.

Pastry

8 oz self-raising flour

5 oz butter

1 tablespoon soft brown sugar

1 beaten egg (or 2 if very small)

Filling

12 oz curd cheese

2 oz caster sugar

2 beaten eggs

Juice of 2 small lemons

Grated rind of 1 lemon

2 teaspoons cornflour

2 tablespoons double cream

2-3 oz raisins, soaked in hot water for 10 minutes then drained

An enormous amount of jam is made in Ambridge during July and August. Strawberry, raspberry, blackcurrant (wonderful with hot water and cinnamon for winter colds) and then damson, plum, and blackberry. Pru Forrest is the champion jam-maker, and her raspberry and redcurrant preserve has won first prize at the Produce Show for many a year. She will not, however, reveal her recipe. Were a gang of international robbers to kidnap husband Tom and threaten to pull his teeth out until the recipe was handed over, I fear he would go toothless through the rest of his days.

Kathy Holland is more generous with her knowledge. I called in at the Bull and found Sid and Lucy gorging themselves on tea scones and raspberry preserve, both provided that afternoon by Kathy. The Borbury fruited scones were still warm from the oven, and the raspberry preserve had a startlingly true taste of fresh fruit about it. Kathy told me later that it was 'freezer jam' – and the easiest thing in the world to make.

Kathy Holland's freezer jam

$1\frac{1}{4}$ lb soft fruit

2 lb caster sugar

$\frac{1}{2}$ bottle liquid pectin (Certo)

2 tablespoons lemon juice

Crush the prepared fruit in a large bowl with the sugar until it is all dissolved. This is simple with raspberries and blackcurrants, but takes longer with strawberries. Leave for an hour, stirring from time to time. Stir in half a bottle of liquid pectin and the lemon juice, and stir thoroughly for 2 or 3 minutes. Decant the jam into small containers (paper cups are ideal) and leave a $\frac{1}{2}$-inch air space before covering with foil. Leave in a warm kitchen for 24 hours. Freeze.

The jam should be used within six months. After defrosting, give it a quick stir before serving. It is wonderful poured over ice-cream!

Borbury fruited tea scones

$\frac{1}{2}$ lb self-raising flour

$1\frac{1}{2}$ oz butter

3 oz dried mixed fruit

Pinch of salt

$\frac{1}{4}$ pint milk

Mix butter into flour and salt until it resembles breadcrumbs. Mix in the dried fruit. Add the milk and mix into a dough – first with a knife and finishing with your fingers. Add a little more milk if it seems dry. Roll out to not less than $\frac{3}{4}$-inch thickness, and cut out the scones. (If you use a small-sized cutter you can eat 3 or 4 scones at a sitting with a clear conscience!) Place on a greased baking tray. Cook in a preheated oven at 220°C (425°F, gas mark 7) for 10-15 minutes. Cool on a wire tray until your will-power runs out, then gobble them up while still warm with butter and freezer jam.

September

RECIPES FOR SEPTEMBER

Tomato, orange and tarragon soup

Hot crab and mushrooms

Eddie Grundy's harvest rabbit casserole

Roast Michaelmas goose with potato stuffing

Hot potato salad

Stuffed sugar plum pastries

Pear and almond tart

Jennifer's spiced blackberry jelly

SEPTEMBER NOTEBOOK

The yellow stubble fields are fringed with corn poppies, yarrow and rosebay willow herb jostle in the country lanes, and a glorious bank of Michaelmas daisies are opening their bright purple heads in Walter Gabriel's garden. But this, somehow, is a month of berries and fruits rather than flowers. In the orchards apples are ripening, and there are glistening blackberries in the hedgerows and up on Lakey Hill. Blackberrying there, on a Sunday afternoon, I sit in the golden autumn sunshine for a while with Brian, who is taking Kate for a walk. The turf is covered with harebells, the most delicious shade of blue. They're the 'bluebells of Scotland' and always remind me of Perthshire.

Most of September's berries have a sinister look. Lords-and-ladies are a vivid, angry red, and stinking iris is a nasty shade of orange. Tom, it turns out, is a bit of an authority on common names for unattractive plants. Feltwort is known as dead men's mittens, and meadow saffron (which I always thought was autumn crocus) is known as naked nannies.

A curious statistic from Elizabeth, whose environmental studies course at Borchester Tech has clearly encompassed a wide range of information. In September there are about $2\frac{1}{2}$ million spiders on every acre of rough grassland. 'If you don't believe me,' she says, 'go out and count them.' She tried to make Nigel do so last year, but he was stung by something after finding only six. 'You've always treated Nigel badly,' says Jill. 'Treat 'em mean, keep 'em keen,' says Elizabeth.

It is the orb spider that spins and weaves such intricate and lovely webs in hedgerow and bramble at this time of year. You can see them best in the early morning, when the sun is coming up and the dew is sparkling and trembling on each gossamer thread. I am endlessly amazed by the intricate pattern and perfect design of every web. Spiders do us no harm whatsoever. Even those that carry poison cannot hurt humans, and they gobble up million upon million of disease-carrying flies and insects.

The swallows are departing from Grey Gables. Swifts went some time ago, just as soon as their fledglings were on the wing, and house martins are still trying to entice their late young from the nest. Now, though, it is the swallows' turn. In the morning they congregate round the chimney pots, and Mr Woolley stares up at them, bewildered. 'Are they hungry? Shall we put out a coconut?' he asks. By mid-afternoon they are chattering, soaring, and swooping round the telephone wires. An hour later, and they are gone. Mr Woolley, putting crumbs on the birdtable, is quite upset. It's as if a large party of guests have complained about the food and stomped off to Redgate Manor or the Cairo Hilton.

Bats from the belfry swoop over the congregation at Evensong. The vicar likes them because they eat up death-watch beetles, but Mrs Perkins is afraid that they will get stuck in her hair. 'It's an old wives' tale,' scoffs Mrs Antrobus, and Mrs Perkins says, 'Well, I'm an old wife and I know what I'm talking about.' Bats hibernate in October, and now they're very busy building up their body fat to see them through the winter.

In the country park the fallow deer are fraying their antlers, a sight that always makes me wince. Every year they grow new antlers under a protective covering of 'velvet', which is a sort of scab. In September the scab becomes itchy, and the bucks thrash against trees and bushes until the velvet is gone, and the new antlers are shiny and hard.

R E C I P E S   F O R   S E P T E M B E R

Calling on Walter, I found him entertaining Mrs Perkins to tea, and regaling her with sliced tongue, lettuce, and Battenberg cake. 'It's all very nice I'm sure, Mr Gabriel,' said Mrs Perkins, 'but where's those special Tiny Tim tomatoes you promised me?' Poor Walter looked evasive and said he'd eaten them all, and Mrs Perkins said he'd have terrible indigestion from the skins. Later, having supper in Nelson's Wine Bar, I found several tiny, sweet tomatoes garnishing my spinach quiche. 'Nelson, how *could* you?' I asked, and Nelson said: 'Dad gets so hurt if I don't let him help me with the business. Anyway, I'm taking him a thermos of Shane's tomato and orange soup in return.'

Shane's soup is excellent, and a good way to use up the glut of tomatoes we often get in September. Shane was reluctant to give me the recipe but Nelson spoke sternly to him, and here it is.

Tomato, orange and tarragon soup

Heat the oil in a pan and gently fry the onion and potato for 5 minutes. Add the tomatoes, tarragon and garlic and stir in the stock and seasoning. Cover and simmer gently for a quarter of an hour. Liquidise or push through a sieve. Stir in the orange juice and zest. Check the seasoning, as it may be necessary to add a pinch of sugar. The soup can be eaten hot with crusty bread, or chilled and served cold with ice cubes and tarragon leaves for decoration.

2 tablespoons sunflower oil

1 medium onion, chopped

1 medium potato, diced

$1\frac{1}{2}$ lb ripe tomatoes, skinned and chopped

2 tablespoons chopped tarragon

1 large clove garlic, crushed

$\frac{1}{2}$ pint light stock

Juice of 2 oranges

1 teaspoon grated orange rind

Freshly ground salt and pepper

Pinch of sugar if necessary

Long, long ago, as a mere child of nineteen, I left Lausanne after a three-month *haute cuisine* cookery course and joined two school friends who were setting up a wine bar in Bristol. It was an amazing venture. Not one of us knew what we were doing, and after a few hectic months one of my friends threw a fit ('I was not put on this earth to mop down tables, cook endless quiches and be nice to drunken *boys*' she screamed one night) and the whole business collapsed, leaving us sadder and very much wiser. One thing I did salvage from the wreck, however, was this recipe for hot crab with mushrooms. Fresh crabs are still available in September, or you can always use frozen crabmeat, and it makes a simple but rather special lunch or first course at a dinner party.

Hot crab and mushrooms

Sauce

1 oz butter

2 tablespoons flour

½ pint milk

1 teaspoon mushroom ketchup

Ingredients

½ lb crabmeat (either white or mixed)

½ lb small button mushrooms

2 slices bread

3 oz butter

Make a sauce by putting the butter, flour, milk and ketchup in a pan and heating gently, stirring all the time until it thickens. Keep warm. Heat 1 oz butter in a frying pan. Add the crabmeat and cook, stirring gently, for 5 minutes. Stir into the sauce. Heat 1 oz butter in the frying pan. Sauté the mushrooms for 1 minute, keeping them on the move all the time. Stir into the sauce. Spoon the crab, mushroom and sauce mixture into 4 ramekins. Make crumbs from the 2 slices of bread and fry them in the remaining 1 oz of butter for 5 minutes or until brown. Place on top of the crab mix and grill the pots of crab until the breadcrumbs are completely brown and crunchy.

If you make this dish in advance for a dinner party, it can be reheated by placing the ramekins into a preheated oven at 180°C (350°F, gas mark 4) for 30 minutes.

There is nothing, according to Jethro, to beat a nice young rabbit split down the middle and fried in bacon fat. 'It makes a breakfast fit for the King of Siam,' he declares, and pesters Clarrie to make Eddie go out and shoot one for him. September is a good time to spot rabbits, when the standing corn is cut and they have fewer places to hide, and there's no denying that a three-quarters grown buck does make a very tasty dish when it's cooked with mushrooms, bacon, and mustard. Rabbits go out to feed at dusk, and Eddie goes out and pots them with his .22 rifle. Then he sells them for a pound each in the Bull. Jethro found him there and asked him for a special discount, and Eddie said, 'All right – twopence,' and Jethro turned red and said, 'Twopence ain't much!' and Eddie said, 'Tell you what, fifty pence and a pint of Shire's,' and Jethro said, 'You must think I'm as daft as ninepence! My eye!'

At Grange Farm, in September, Clarrie makes Eddie's favourite rabbit casserole. 'In fact,' she says, 'I make it over and over till I'm sick of rabbit. But Eddie never is, and neither is Joe, and even William gobbles it up like nobody's business.' As one might expect, Shire's traditional ale is a vital ingredient in Eddie's favourite dish, but if Shire's is not obtainable in your part of the world you can substitute any strong dark bitter beer.

In September Clarrie puts courgettes into the pot, but later in the year she substitutes parsnips, turnips, and swede.

Eddie Grundy's harvest rabbit casserole

Joint the rabbit and coat well in seasoned flour. Fry the joints in oil until golden brown, then place in a casserole. Slice and fry the onion, and add to the rabbit. Add sliced courgettes and carrots. Add the beef stock, beer and bouquet garni. Cover, and cook at 180°C (350°F, gas mark 4) until rabbit is tender – about 1½ to 2 hours. Serve with mashed potatoes and accompanied by several more pints of Shire's bitter.

Ingredients
1 rabbit
2 oz seasoned flour
A little oil for frying
1 large onion
2 courgettes (or more, depending on size)
2 large carrots
½ pint beef stock
½ pint Shire's traditional bitter
Bouquet garni

Tom said to me: 'If I was to stand in the church porch early in the morning and ring a bell and shout, "Badger's Bank! Wormitts! Upper Parks!" you'd say I'd gone mad.' I had to agree that such behaviour would seem peculiar, and Tom said, 'That's what churchwardens had to do in the old days, believe it or not.'

He was talking about the churchwardens' job in Victorian times, calling the names of individual fields for village women to go gleaning in after harvest. Labourers' families were so poor that some women would go out at the break of dawn to reach the fields first, and sometimes go into fields where the corn was only half cut. Eventually a rule was made: no field could be entered until the churchwarden had announced, from the church porch, that it was open for the gleaners.

After the village women came the best gleaners of all – the village geese. They waddled through the stubble, fattening themselves on whatever spilt grain was left, and by the time they had finished it was truly possible to say that the harvest was 'gathered in'. The geese gorged themselves until Michaelmas, and then they were killed and eaten, and each village family would store up jars of goosefat to use as revolting medicaments and 'rubs' as a protection against winter colds and chills.

In Ambridge the roast goose was traditionally cooked with a potato stuffing (to soak up the fat and make the meat go further!) and this stuffing, with its diced bacon, sausagemeat, and herbs, is a delight in itself!

Roast Michaelmas goose with potato stuffing

8 lb goose

1 lemon

6 large potatoes (cooked and mashed with as little butter and milk as possible)

1 large onion, chopped

4 oz streaky bacon (cut in one piece then diced)

1 lb pork sausagemeat

1 tablespoon chopped parsley

1 teaspoon each of chopped thyme and sage

Freshly ground salt and pepper

Take the goose and prick the skin all over. Rub with the cut lemon, but keep back a little of the juice to squeeze inside the bird. Sprinkle the skin generously with salt and pepper. For the stuffing: thoroughly mix together the potato, chopped onion, bacon and sausagemeat. Add the fresh herbs and seasoning. Stuff the goose firmly and secure the opening with a small skewer. Place the bird on its breast on a rack over a roasting tin in a preheated oven at 220°C (425°F, gas mark 7) for half an hour. Reduce the heat to 180°C (350°F, gas mark 4) and cook for a further 3 hours, turning the bird over from time to time, and occasionally emptying the excess fat from the roasting tin. The goose should be cooked until almost all the fat has been shed, and the skin is crisp.

Two wonderful accompaniments to roast goose are onion sauce – also famous with lamb, of course – and apple sauce. Here are Borsetshire recipes for both.

Onion sauce

Place the onions, turnip, milk and water in a pan. Bring to the boil and simmer until the onions are very soft. Remove from the heat and mash with the butter, seasoning and nutmeg until smooth. Keep warm and stir in the cream when ready to serve.

4 medium onions, chopped
$\frac{1}{4}$ pint water
$\frac{1}{4}$ pint milk
An inch-thick slice of turnip, diced
2 oz butter
4 tablespoons single cream
$\frac{1}{2}$ teaspoon freshly grated nutmeg
Freshly ground salt and pepper

Apple sauce

Peel, core and chop the apples and put in a pan with the cider. Cook until the apples have pulped. Stir in the butter, sugar, lemon juice and salt. Keep hot until ready to serve.

2 large cooking apples (Lord Derby, or the first of the Bramleys)
$\frac{1}{4}$ pint dry cider
1 oz butter
2 tablespoons sugar
Juice of half a lemon
Small pinch of salt

'We'll soon be able to have potatoes in their jackets again,' said Shula dreamily, 'with big blobs of butter in them. And potatoes *boulangère* with black pepper and cream, and mashed potatoes with even more butter and cream . . . no wonder I can never lose weight!'

It isn't the much-maligned potato, of course, that causes the trouble, it's the stuff we eat with them. This recipe is rather healthy – particularly if you use sunflower oil – and is a good way of using potatoes that are not exactly *new* and not exactly *old*. It goes down very well at a late-season barbecue when there is a chill in the air, and cold potato salad has lost its appeal!

Hot potato salad

Ingredients
1-1½ lb potatoes
1 onion, thinly sliced
6 tablespoons sunflower or olive oil
1 tablespoon cider
1 tablespoon wine vinegar
1 teaspoon mustard
2 cloves garlic, crushed
Freshly ground salt and pepper
Chopped parsley for garnish

Scrub the potatoes and cook them in boiling, salted water until just tender. In another pan heat half the oil and cook the onion and garlic for a few minutes. Add the remaining oil, cider and vinegar. Stir in the mustard and seasoning and heat until boiling. Drain the cooked potatoes and put them in the hot dressing. If they are small, just stir them in, if larger chop them in the dressing. Sprinkle with parsley and serve hot.

There are plum trees and damson trees in all the old cottage gardens, many of them ancient and long past their best ('Just like I am,' says Walter mournfully) but generally regarded as old friends who, year after year, offer up a bounty of yellow and purple fruit. The sweetest plum tree in Ambridge is said to be a sort of Victoria that grows in the garden of the police house, and Detective-Sergeant Barry was shocked to find Mrs Perkins raiding it one afternoon. 'You're stealing my plums!' he cried in outrage, and Mrs Perkins said she'd always had 'an arrangement' to use police-house plums to make jam for the church's Christmas bazaar. 'If you and Miss Holland were married perhaps you'd both be here instead of always over at her cottage in Penny Hassett and then perhaps she'd make the jam for the church bazaar and I wouldn't have to stand over a hot stove at my age.'

Dave let her have the plums – but insisted she give him a jar of jam in return. He also let me have a dozen (they really are the fattest, juiciest I've ever seen) so that I could make one of my favourite autumn puddings – hot plums stuffed with almonds and brown sugar and encased in Jean Paul's special sweet shortcrust pastry.

Stuffed sugar plum pastries

1 lb self-raising flour	
10 oz butter	
2 tablespoons soft brown sugar	
3 eggs, beaten	
12 ripe plums	
2 oz soft brown sugar	
4 oz flaked almonds	
Milk and caster sugar for glaze	

Make the pastry in the usual way and roll out thinly. Cut open the plums and remove the stones. Chop the almonds up with the soft brown sugar. Stuff the plums with this mixture. Place the plums on the pastry. Cut the pastry and wrap round each plum. Place the pastry-wrapped plums in a buttered dish after brushing them with milk and sprinkling with caster sugar (12 plums will fit neatly into an 11-by-7-inch Swiss roll tin). Bake for half an hour in a preheated oven at 200°C (400°F, gas mark 6). Serve hot with pouring cream.

The first pears are ripening in the orchards of the Vale of Am, and when I drive home to Darrington for the weekend I eagerly watch the blackboard-sign outside a farm-shop near Loxley Barratt. In August it announces Discovery and Tydemans Early apples. In September it proclaims 'Vic Plums', Worcester Permain and Lord Derby apples, and towards the end of the month the first Conference pears. Eaten when just ripe they have a crisp, nutty flavour which mellows if you ripen them still further at home. They are also splendid for cooking, and this pear tart is Jill Archer's favourite dinner-party pud.

It should be served still warm from the oven, with chilled cream.

Pear and almond tart

Pastry

8 oz self-raising flour

5 oz butter

1 tablespoon brown sugar

1 medium egg, beaten

Filling

5 dessert pears

4 oz vanilla sugar

8 fl oz water

1 lemon

4 oz butter

4 oz caster sugar

2 eggs, beaten

4 oz ground almonds

Make the pastry and roll it out to line a 7-inch flan dish or tin. Preheat the oven to 180°C (350°F, gas mark 4) and bake the pastry blind for 15 minutes, preferably on a baking tray. Remove from the oven and turn the temperature down to 170°C (325°F, gas mark 3). Prepare the pears by peeling, halving, and poaching them for five minutes in a sugar syrup made from the water, vanilla sugar, and grated peel of half the lemon. (To make this dissolve the sugar in the water and simmer with the peel for 5 minutes.) For the filling, cream the butter and caster sugar, and beat in, singly, the 2 eggs and the juice of the lemon. Mix in the ground almonds. Spread the mixture over the partly cooked flan case and arrange the drained pear halves in a sunray pattern on top. Bake for 30 minutes or until set. Place tin foil on the edge of the pastry if it seems in danger of burning.

30 September is Kate Aldridge's birthday, and Jennifer always lays on a superb party for her at Home Farm, with a magician, a video film, and masses to eat and drink (including sherry and home-made cheese straws for the Mums). 'The trouble is, though,' she moans, 'that all the children want to eat is sausages and crisps and baked beans and ice-cream. They don't like anything unless it's stuffed to bursting with preservatives and E-additives. Show them some revolting snackette made out of salt, sugar, and mono-sodium glutamate, and they go for it like ferrets up a drainpipe.' 'Like *what?*' asks Brian, astonished. 'You know what I mean,' says Jennifer. 'I've tried to entice their tastebuds with wholemeal scones and celery bits with cream cheese, but they just turn nasty and take it out on Kate when I'm not looking.'

This year sausages on sticks, and crisps, and bought ice-cream featured strongly on the party menu – but Jennifer did have one triumph. Her home-made spiced blackberry jelly was wolfed down by every child. 'Not one of them suspected it was free from E-additives,' said Jennifer proudly.

Jennifer's spiced blackberry jelly

1 lb apples, peeled, cored, sliced and weighed after preparation

1 lb blackberries

3 oz sugar

1 teaspoon ground cinnamon

1 oz (2 sachets) gelatine

4 fl oz hot water

Place the fruit, sugar and cinnamon in a pan and heat slowly to boiling point. Simmer for a quarter of an hour. Sprinkle the gelatine into the hot water and when dissolved satisfactorily stir briskly. Rub the cooked fruit through a sieve and add the gelatine mixture. Pour into a wetted 1-pint mould and leave to set in the refrigerator – preferably overnight.

October

RECIPES FOR OCTOBER

Ambridge harvest soup

Stilton and apples in flaky pastry

Roast hand of pork with watercress stuffing

Courgette and mushroom salad

Pigeon breasts in red wine with gooseberry sauce

Apple, blackberry and almond pie

Hazelnut and Marsala ice-cream

Ginger pears

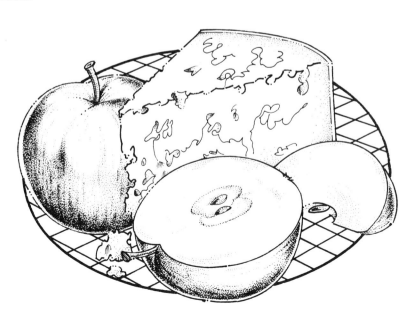

O C T O B E R   N O T E B O O K

One day it is still summer: fields and footpaths are fringed with clover and yellow ragwort, butterflies flap idly among the garden flowers – the bright orange calendulas and vivid blue gentians – and the sun pours down from a clear sky as the early mists evaporate. Then, next morning, the dahlias are blackened with frost, bonfire smoke drifts on the cold air, and it is autumn.

Ambridge Harvest Festival is on the second Sunday of the month. The corn harvest is over in September, but Brian's beet harvest has only just started, they're still lifting potatoes at Brookfield, and it's well into October before Carol Treggoran can pick her Cox's apples at the market garden. The church is packed. There are chrysanthemums and corn sheaves round the pulpit, rose-red apples and early turnips along the stone window-sills. Joe Grundy watches them with a wary eye. His grandfather, he claims, was stunned by a toppling mangel wurzel in 1935.

This is the month of the wild harvest, the fruits of field and hedgerow. Blackbirds scoff mountain ash berries, and in the country park the deer crunch up conkers and will soon be foraging for acorns and crab apples. Rabbits generally get to the delicious apricot-scented chanterelle mushrooms before I can, and one morning by the lake I find Martha Woodford collecting fat, purple sloes (for her famous sloe gin!) and Colonel Danby stuffing handfuls of filbert nuts into his overcoat pockets. They both look horribly guilty when I pounce on them from behind an oak.

Captain finds a hedgehog, also out foraging for winter supplies, and Tom comes up and says: 'Good Captain! That's the first useful thing you've done in years!' He wants to kill the hedgehog but I won't let him. 'I don't care what you city folk reckon,' Tom declares stoutly (even more stoutly than usual after a double helping of upside-down pudding at lunchtime), 'but hedgehogs eat my pheasant eggs and that's something I won't allow.'

'I'm as country-born as you are,' I tell him, 'and I don't care if they do snaffle the odd egg. They also eat slugs and beetles and they never did us any harm.'

Tom wasn't satisfied. Shula told me that in the Bull he was grumbling to Joe Grundy, who shares his prejudice against the hedgehog. Joe believes the old country story about hedgehogs 'milking' cows by suckling on them when they are asleep. Even Tom is doubtful about this. 'I'm not saying hedgehogs won't lap a bit of milk that's leaked out of the udder,' he says, but Joe is firm. 'You should see my poor sore cows after some prickly hedgehog snout's been nuzzling their teats.'

By the end of the month all the hedgehogs are safely tucked up in hibernation, breathing once every five minutes or so, and dreaming, no doubt, of Tom's pheasant eggs and Joe Grundy's creamy milk.

Birds are recovering from their moult, and sing with new vigour, the robin loudly claiming its territorial rights and the tiny wren warbling away with great ferocity. At night the brown owl makes his smooth, chocolatey-deep call through the autumn woods. He, too, has a new set of feathers to warm him, as he glides in the moonlight, his sharp amber eyes searching for the movement of field mice and little creatures in the fields beneath.

R E C I P E S   F O R   O C T O B E R

The Harvest Supper is a grand village get–together, with upwards of a hundred people sitting down to cold ham and beef with salad, baked potatoes, and apple and black-berry pie with cream. The pies are baked by different women, and there is often discreet manoeuvring to secure a slice made by a noted pastrycook! It's a very jolly occasion with the farmers in their best check sports jackets and fawn corduroys, and the elderly ladies of the village always, for some curious reason, eating with their hats and coats on. Afterwards Tom Forrest entertains everyone with old Borsetshire folk songs like 'Jim the Carter's Lad' and 'The Village Pump', and a great deal of beer and cider is consumed.

A couple of years ago Nelson Gabriel provided a wonderful cider cup made out of 12 pints dry cider, 3 pints ginger ale, 8 fl oz of Grand Marnier, and lots of orange, lemon, and cherry bits (serve it straight away, before all the ginger ale bubbles disappear). I was sitting next to Mr Fletcher from Glebelands, who owns a paint factory in Felpersham, and opposite Dan Archer who was born at Brookfield Farm in 1896. 'You're a man of the land you are, Dan,' said Mr Fletcher, after three glasses of cider cup. 'You'll be remembering the old harvest home when the reaping was finished, and the corn dolly was borne back in triumph, and the harvest wain was decorated with boughs of oak and ash, and the horses were garlanded and the men rode on top dressed as women.' Dan thought for a moment, then said, 'No, I don't remember any of that. A fiddler did come to Brookfield once, but I think that was at Christmas.'

Anyway, the Ambridge Harvest Supper starts with a thick vegetable soup enriched with cheddar cheese – perfect for a chilly autumn night when the heating in the village hall has broken down!

Ambridge harvest soup

(serves 10 people)
1 cauliflower
3 large leeks
3 large potatoes
2 pints chicken stock
$\frac{1}{2}$ teaspoon grated nutmeg
$1\frac{3}{4}$ pints milk
4 oz mature Cheddar cheese, grated
Freshly ground salt and pepper
Finely chopped parsley for garnish

Break the cauliflower into sprigs, slice the leeks, peel and cut the potatoes into chunks. Place in a saucepan with the stock, seasoning, and the nutmeg. Bring to the boil. Simmer for about half an hour. Sieve or liquidise until smooth. Reheat, adding the milk. Remove from the heat and stir in the cheese until it has melted. Serve garnished with chopped parsley.

October brings the apple crop to its full glory. Worcester Pearmain and Tydemans Early ripened in September, but now come the most delicious, juicy, fully flavoured apples of all – Cox's Orange Pippin, and the crisp Egremont Russet. This last apple, with its distinctive brown skin, is sometimes hard to get hold of – which is frustrating when I want to taste its distinctive nutty flavour in this apple and stilton gourmet starter. Jethro Larkin has an old Russet tree, which yields a few pounds of fruit each year, but he is very unwilling to hand any over. 'Cook my Russets in pastry?' he exclaims, 'You don't want to do that! You go and use some Bramleys and a bit of sugar. Cook Russets? My eye!'

Russets can be cooked, though, and this dish is a great favourite with Mr Woolley's friend the Admiral. He knows we often have it on the menu at this time of year (supply of apples permitting) and is a frequent visitor for lunch. The Admiral not only starts his meal with it, he has also been known to demand it for pudding – and has gobbled it up with thick cream.

Stilton and apples in flaky pastry

Put the margarine into the freezer, and when frozen grate into the sifted flour and salt. Add enough liquid to make a workable dough. Put in a polythene bag and chill in the fridge for at least half an hour. Peel, core and chop the apples into small cubes. Place in a bowl. Sprinkle with the juice of the lemon. Crumble the stilton over the apple cubes. Add the thyme leaves and nutmeg to taste. Mix well and add a little pepper. Roll the pastry out into a thin square, approximately 12 inches by 12 inches. Cover two-thirds of the pastry with the apple and cheese mix. Roll up, towards the empty pastry, in the manner of a Swiss roll. When completely rolled up, seal the ends and place on a greased baking sheet, keeping the join in the pastry underneath. Brush with a little milk and cook in a preheated oven at 180°C (350°F, gas mark 4) for 30-35 minutes. Serve hot.

Pastry
8 oz plain flour
6 oz hard margarine
Pinch of salt
Cold water
Filling
1 lb Russet apples (or Cox's will do)
$\frac{1}{2}$ lb stilton
1 lemon
Sprig of fresh thyme
Freshly grated nutmeg
Freshly ground black pepper
A little milk

At one time, every cottager in Ambridge kept a pig, fattening it up during the summer and calling in the pig-sticker to kill it some time during October or November. Walter Gabriel remembers how his father was more fond of his pigs than anything (including Walter), and kept them in a very luxurious sty at the bottom of the garden, feeding them on barley and parsnips. He would only call in Piggy Atkins (the pig-sticker) if the moon was on the wane, and he would be near to tears when the moment came. But, Walter says, it was all well worth it. A countrywoman could get an astounding amount of food out of an average-size pig. Apart from the joints, the hams, and the bacon, there would be sausages and pork pies, brawn, chitterlings and faggots, pig's pudding and saveloys, at least 20 lb of beautiful lard and handfuls of crunchy pork scratchings!

Leg of pork is generally considered the prime cut for a roast, but I much prefer the hand, with its sweet, juicy meat and its superb crackling. At Blossom Hill Cottage, Peggy Archer serves it with a delicious watercress stuffing.

Roast hand of pork with watercress stuffing

Hand of pork (approx 5½ lb)
Juniper berries
2 onions
2 bunches of watercress
Grated rind of a lemon
2 oz fresh breadcrumbs
Freshly ground salt and pepper
Pinch of ground nutmeg
1 egg, beaten
1 tablespoon lemon juice

Ask the butcher to score the skin and cut a pocket on the underside near the bone. To make the stuffing, finely chop the onions and drop into boiling water for 5 minutes. Chop the watercress leaves and stalks. Mix the onion, watercress and remaining ingredients in a bowl and stuff into the pocket in the meat. Make sure the skin is dry and then sprinkle with a thin coating of salt. Press the juniper berries into the slits in the skin. Cook for 2½ hours in a preheated oven at 230°C (450°F, gas mark 8).

Heavy rain for a couple of days is followed by clear skies, and in the soggy undergrowth round Arkwright Lake I find the most fantastic fungi creations, weirdly sprouting from rotting, dead tree trunks, while Scarlet Cap with its red top and white spots is scattered over a woodland glade. Most fungi (but certainly not Scarlet Cap!) is good to eat, and George Barford is always pointing at suspicious-looking growths and calling them blewits. But on my own I am never *quite* sure and usually end up pinching a few ordinary button mushrooms from the kitchen. Then I go to the kitchen garden in search of some late courgettes, manage to grab some before Higgs has time to complain, and make a super courgette and mushroom salad to have with cold ham for lunch. The following ingredients are for four people.

Courgette and mushroom salad

Place everything except the mushrooms and courgettes in a bowl and blend together with a fork. Blanch the courgettes, drain, and pat dry with kitchen paper. Mix with the mushrooms. Add the dressing immediately. Toss, then chill before serving.

3 tablespoons olive oil
1½ tablespoons lemon juice
½ tablespoon tarragon vinegar
½ level teaspoon sugar
½ level teaspoon mustard
1 clove garlic, crushed
½ tablespoon chopped mint
¾ lb courgettes, sliced
6 oz small button mushrooms

David Archer and Eddie Grundy meet for a pint in the Bull before going pigeon-shooting. Wood pigeons, David says, are not only rapacious but are infinitely cunning and sly. That is why both he and Eddie are wearing ex-army camouflage jackets and khaki woollen hats. Sid Perks admires the dedicated way in which Eddie has streaked dirt on his face, but Eddie only glowers and asks Sid if he's trying to be funny. Sometimes David puts decoy pigeons (stool-pigeons, in fact!) into a crop to tempt birds down to a field where he is hiding; sometimes he, Eddie, and Brian stake themselves out in different woods and shoot the flocks of birds as they wheel about from one 'safe' harbour to another. As winter sets in more and more growing crops will be raided: cauliflower and kale, cabbage, oilseed rape, and even grazing clover; and more and more pigeons, of course, will pay the price!

At Grey Gables Hereford pigeon pie is a favourite bar meal in winter, and is very simple to make. (2 jointed pigeons, 12 oz stewing steak, 2 diced carrots and 2 diced onions should be covered in water, seasoned, and simmered for 2½ hours. The meat and vegetables should then be taken from the liquid, placed in a pie dish with a little liquid added, covered with 6 oz shortcrust pastry, and cooked for a further 30 minutes until golden brown at 375°F (190°C, gas mark 5).) In the restaurant, though, we serve a very special dish in October, when pigeons are plump, tender, and at their very best after feasting on the crops of summer and autumn. Served in this way, pigeon is fit for the most splendid of dinner parties.

Pigeon breasts in red wine with gooseberry sauce

4 plump pigeons

1 tablespoon gooseberry jelly (or crab apple)

Marinade

2 tablespoons olive oil

1 carrot

1 onion

1 stick celery

Piece of fennel bulb

Parsley stalks

3 cloves garlic

Freshly ground salt

Black peppercorns

$\frac{1}{4}$ teaspoon cumin seeds

$\frac{1}{4}$ pint red wine

To make the marinade: gently heat the olive oil in a saucepan. Roughly chop the onion, celery, carrot, fennel, parsley and garlic, and add to the oil. Cook until the onions begin to turn golden brown. Add the salt, peppercorns, and cumin seeds. Add the wine and bring to the boil. Reduce slightly. Remove from heat and cool. While the marinade is cooling, remove the pigeon breasts, dry, and place in a bowl. Chop the carcases roughly and brown in a frying pan. Cover with water to make a strong stock. When the marinade has cooled, pour it over the pigeon breasts and stand in the fridge overnight. Remove the pigeon breasts from the marinade and dry them. Strain the marinade and keep on one side for the sauce.

Heat a non-stick frying pan and sear the pigeon breasts on the skin side. Reduce the heat after a minute or so and cook for a further 5 minutes. Raise the heat and repeat the process on the other side of the pigeon breasts. A slightly shorter time and the pigeons will be rare in the centre, a little longer and they will be well done. They are at their nicest, I think, when still a bit pink. Remove from the pan and keep warm. Keep the frying pan hot and add the strained marinade, the fruit jelly, and 6 tablespoons of pigeon stock. Boil fiercely until the sauce is syrupy. Slice the pigeon breasts, and serve with the sauce and a green vegetable.

The old country saying is that the devil spits on blackberries at Michaelmas and turns them woody and nasty to eat. If it's been a late season, though, blackberries can be at their very best in the early part of October. This time of year is known as 'St Luke's Little Summer' because the weather is so often sunny and warm for a few days before the wild autumn gales set in. Christine Barford says she almost always uses October blackberries for the apple and blackberry pie she makes for the Harvest Supper – and she cooks the fruit in a special almond shortcrust pastry.

Place the ingredients for the pastry in a bowl. Blend together to form a dough. Knead, then cover and chill for one hour. Place the apples in a 1½-pint pie dish together with the blackberries and biscuits, and sprinkle with sugar. Roll out the pastry and cover the fruit. Decorate with leaves made from the pastry trimmings, brush with milk and sprinkle with sugar. Bake at 190°C (375°F, gas mark 5) for 35-40 minutes.

Apple, blackberry and almond pie

Pastry

6 oz plain flour

3 oz softened butter

2 oz ground almonds

1 oz caster sugar

1 lightly beaten egg

Filling

1½ lb Bramley apples, peeled, cored and sliced

8 oz blackberries

3 oz ratafia biscuits

1 oz caster sugar

Milk and sugar for glaze

A little nuthatch seizes a hazelnut from the tree by the old coachhouse, darts over to a favourite gatepost, jams the nut into a crack in the wood, and starts to tap furiously at the shell. Soon bits of shell and soft kernel are flying in all directions, and a lazy jay, resplendent in her autumn feathers, comes and prods around in the fallen leaves for bits of discarded nut. Mr Woolley sighs and shakes his head. 'Workers and drones, Caroline,' he says. 'That jay might preen herself in her finery, but it's the poor little nuthatch that's doing all the work. It's a lesson for us all.' Under the hazelnut tree are numerous empty shells, some with perfect round holes gnawed in them by dormice, others split wide open by grey squirrels. Nuts of all kinds – acorns, hazels, even conkers – are the iron rations that many small animals and birds depend on during the hard winter months. I hope they don't begrudge me a few nuts myself, to make this mouth-wateringly delicious and splendidly rich ice-cream dessert.

Hazelnut and Marsala ice-cream

4 oz shelled hazelnuts

1 pint double cream

½ pint single cream

4 oz sugar

4 egg yolks, well beaten

2 generous tablespoons of Marsala

Chop the unskinned nuts finely and toast them on a baking tray in a moderate oven at 180°C (350°F, gas mark 4). Put the nuts in a saucepan with the cream and bring very slowly to the boil. Simmer very gently for 5 minutes. Take the pan off the heat and stir in the sugar and the well beaten egg yolks. Return to the heat and cook very gently until the mixture thickens. Be careful not to let it boil. Cool, stirring constantly. Add the Marsala. Put into a plastic container and freeze until the mix has frozen half an inch in from the edge of the container. Remove from the freezer, put in a bowl, and whisk to break up the ice crystals. Return to container and freeze. Place in fridge for half an hour before serving.

Tom and Pru Forrest live in a small woodman's cottage (which is quite a different thing from the cottage of a small woodman!) near to Lyttleton Covert. The cottage was built in the sixties by the estate owner, Ralph Bellamy, and when Tom and Pru moved in they were given a young pear tree as a housewarming gift, and planted it in the middle of their lawn. Now in its full glory, and well protected from springtime frosts, the tree gives a bountiful harvest almost every year. Pru is an enterprising cook who often tires of making interminable suet puddings for Tom, and a couple of years ago she entered this recipe for ginger pears in a WI competition – it won first prize. It was entered as a party recipe, so please note that the quantities are for ten people!

Ginger pears

1½ pints dry white wine

½ pint ginger wine

8 oz caster sugar

2 lemons (the juice and pared rind)

10 dessert pears

Stem ginger, thinly sliced

Mix together in a saucepan with a tight-fitting lid the white wine, ginger wine, sugar, lemon juice and rind. Bring to the boil to dissolve the sugar. Boil rapidly for a few minutes until syrupy. Meanwhile, use a potato-peeler or small, sharp knife to carefully peel a spiral of skin from each pear, like a helter-skelter, starting at the top of the fruit and working round it to the base. (This is for decorative purposes only – leave most of the skin on!) Leave the stalks on the fruit. Place in the syrup and poach on a low heat for 20 minutes or until tender. Serve in a shallow dish with the pears upright and syrup poured over them. Decorate the stalks with stem ginger to resemble leaves.

November

RECIPES FOR NOVEMBER

Brussels sprouts with chestnuts

Edgeley leek and bacon pie

Victorian sprout and ham soup

Nigel's scrambled eggs with smoked salmon

Fillet of venison 'Grey Gables'

Crispy pork and haricot bean casserole

Clarrie Grundy's oat and apple cake

A plum pudding with barley wine

Pear chutney

NOVEMBER NOTEBOOK

Nobody seems to like November – except me! I love to exercise Ivor on dank, foggy afternoons, when lights shine from cottage windows by four o'clock, the smell of autumn is in the air, and my head is full of thoughts about crumpets with melted butter. Then there are those crisp, silent mornings after a frost when nothing in the woodland moves – until a squirrel darts along a branch and huge sycamore leaves float down through the still air.

I take Captain for walks along the woodland rides, scuffing the dead leaves with my feet and kicking them up into the air. Captain pretends to jump up and catch them, which is sporting of him. Tom plods out from behind a holly tree thick with green berries, shakes his head at us, and mutters, 'Oh dear, oh dear.' He gives the impression that someone is going to have to come along and tidy the leaves up behind us. He does not approve of frivolous behaviour near the shoot just as the pheasant season is starting. I listen politely while he grumbles about poachers and predators and scoffs at grey squirrels. 'And if you think squirrels are clever enough to hoard little piles of nuts and berries for the winter you're wrong,' he says. 'It's the industrious woodmouse that stores up a food larder. Squirrels just bury a nut here and a nut there – it beats me how they ever find them again!'

Stray summer flowers linger on in cottage gardens, but the November delight is the hedgerow, resplendent with the bright, shiny, scarlet hips of the dog rose, and the dark red haws of the hawthorn. Then there is Old Man's Beard, fluffy and white and spangled with moisture. They call it Gypsy Tobacco in some parts, because the dry stem can (goodness knows how!) be smoked in a pipe.

I feel sorry for the tiny shrew, spotted for a moment darting through a pile of dead chestnut leaves, then gone except for a single high-pitched squeak. One of his cousins, the hedgehog, is comfortably asleep by now, and another, the mole, is burrowing through the still-warm earth, but the defenceless shrew must somehow struggle on as the weather turns cold and food becomes scarce. Shrews have a very short life, and spend most of it rushing about in search of insects to eat, stopping now and then to fall asleep for a few minutes, then rushing about some more. They never live for more than one winter. Owls eat them in great numbers. Foxes and cats kill them, but then spit them out, disliking the taste. Being nasty to eat is the poor little shrew's only way of getting its own back on the world.

A creature I have no sympathy with is the stoat. Childhood memories of horrible stoat-soldiers in *The Wind in the Willows* come vividly to mind as I watch young rabbits cropping the grass in the early morning. Towards them, like a writhing snake, comes a bitch stoat with six or seven kittens. At this time of year she is teaching them how to kill, and they are imitating her every move. The terrible thing is that she has selected which rabbit is her prey, and the victim somehow knows that she has been selected – and that she is doomed. She sits, petrified, waiting to be killed, and the other rabbits, who know that this time they are safe, carry on cropping the grass for breakfast.

RECIPES FOR NOVEMBER

Sprouts are grown on the farms round Perivale-on-Edge, thriving for some reason on the higher, more exposed land. Last year one farmer was astonished to wake up and find that a gang of sprout-robbers had descended during the night, and stripped bare a twenty-acre field. He reckoned they must have been the most dedicated, hard-working thieves in history! Perhaps, though, they just relished eating young baby sprouts that had been sweetened by the first frosts of winter. They might even have discovered this recipe for sprouts sautéed with chestnuts, and been too excited to wait until the shops opened.

Brussels sprouts with chestnuts

1 lb Brussels sprouts	
8 oz chestnuts	
Freshly ground salt and pepper	
3 oz butter	
Pinch of nutmeg	

Place the chestnuts in water and bring to the boil. Take out of the water and peel. Put the peeled chestnuts in boiling water and cook for 15 minutes. Drain. Melt the butter in a pan and sauté the chestnuts for about 5 minutes. Add to this the sprouts, which have been cooked in boiling, salted water for 6 minutes. Sauté the sprouts and the chestnuts together for a further minute. Tip into a serving dish and sprinkle with a little nutmeg and pepper.

When I go to the kitchen garden to ask Higgs if the leeks are ready to lift, he grumbles about pigeons on his Savoy cabbages, maggots in his July-sown carrots, and slugs in his celery trench. Over our heads a flock of fieldfares, newly arrived after their long migration from the continent, wheel and turn before coming to rest in the woods by the lake. Higgs says he hasn't time to admire the beauties of nature, not when he's double-digging his potato patch and being asked to provide leeks every five minutes.

Later, in the village shop, Martha gives me a recipe for leek and bacon pie that originated in the tiny hamlet of Edgeley, two miles from Ambridge on the Borchester Road. 'They were poor people in Edgeley,' says Martha, 'notable because they couldn't even afford a bit of bacon in their pie.' I point out that you can't have bacon in everything, and Joe Grundy, who is hovering by the birthday cards, says, 'Yes you can, if you want to,' and Bill Insley says, 'Well, what about trifle?' and Joe says, 'We never had trifle when I was a lad.' It turns out that Edgeley's *famous* pie was devised when the turnpike opened, and the cottagers because suddenly prosperous, and could afford to put more bacon in their pie than anybody else!

Edgeley leek and bacon pie

1–2 oz butter
2 lb or so of potatoes, cooked and mashed
3 or 4 leeks, chopped
3 or 4 thick rashers of bacon
Grated cheese

Sweat the leeks in a little butter for about ten minutes, and at the same time fry up the bacon rashers until they are nice and crispy. Line a dish with the leeks and lay the rashers across them. Top the leek and bacon mix with mashed potato, and cover with lots of grated cheese. Place under the grill and brown. This makes a lovely warming supper on a damp November evening!

According to Mrs Marjorie Antrobus, sprout and ham soup was a great favourite of Prince Albert and was only served to Queen Victoria once after his death, upon which occasion she refused to speak through the rest of the meal and greatly offended the special commissioner from the American Confederacy. In order to placate the commissioner from the newly emergent cotton state the Foreign Office is supposed to have allowed the construction of the Confederate cruiser *Alabama* at Birkenhead, which subsequently did £3 million worth of damage to Yankee shipping – a sum of money which the British government was forced to repay in 1872. 'Nobody knows whether Queen Victoria was silent in memory of the Prince Consort,' said Mrs Antrobus, 'or whether the chef failed to add the proper amount of grated nutmeg. It shows what can happen if we are careless with our ingredients.'

This soup has a beautiful colour and a lovely, tangy flavour, and it is easy to see why the Victorians, including Prince Albert, enjoyed it so much.

Victorian sprout and ham soup

Heat the butter in a saucepan and sweat the onions gently for about 10 minutes. Add the sprouts and 2 oz finely chopped ham. Stir over a gentle heat for a few minutes and then season and sprinkle with nutmeg and flour. Gradually add the stock and bring to the boil. Simmer for 5 minutes. Liquidise (or sieve) and return to the heat. Add the remaining 2 oz ham, cut into strips. Stir in the cream. Heat through gently and adjust the seasoning.

2 oz butter
4 oz lean ham
1 small onion, finely chopped
12 oz sprouts, finely sliced
Freshly ground salt and pepper
$\frac{1}{4}$ nutmeg, freshly grated
1 tablespoon plain flour
2 pints light stock
$\frac{1}{4}$ pint single cream

A clear November morning with a keen scent brings fifty mounted and twice that many on foot to the opening meet of the South Borset Hunt outside the Bull. Sid Perks weaves his way through the crowd with a tray of drinks, Shula has a new black jacket and shining boots and is mounted on Carroway (she's taken the morning off work!) and Tom is all ready to follow the sport in his van. It is a colourful and good-humoured scene, for hunting runs through country life like a wick through a candle. We move off, hounds find in a covert on Home Farm land, the fox sets his mask for Ten Elms Rise, and we are away! Hours later I hack back along the lanes with Shula, both of us bone-weary, splattered in mud, and totally content. Ahead lie scrambled eggs and pots of hot tea in front of a log fire at Brookfield.

Nigel Pargetter hunted with the South Borset on many a glorious day last season, and although not exactly a master chef he certainly knows how to run up a pretty mean scrambled egg. He even gave me the recipe, together with his helpful hints!

HELPFUL HINT ONE: Underwoods' Food Hall, where liveth the fearful old dragon who sacked me for nibbling venison pie, stocks 1 lb packs of smoked salmon bits designed specially for blokes like me who tend to be on their financial uppers. They're the scraps from the rich man's table, of course, but just the job for eating with scrambled eggs.

HELPFUL HINT TWO: If you do grab a pack from the wizened crone you can use the salmon bits to make faces on the scrambled eggs – i.e. Mr Happy or Mr Sad. It takes a long time, though, to write 'I love Lizzie', and the eggs go cold.

Nigel's scrambled eggs with smoked salmon

3 eggs per person
2 oz smoked salmon per person
Butter (lots of)
White bread
Black pepper
Malt whisky (lots and lots of)

Shove a blob of butter into a pan, bung it on the heat and swirl it round till it froths up. Into the foam cast the thoroughly beaten eggs. Stir like mad with a wooden spoon, but take it off while it is still a bit yolky – if it goes pale yellow and dry throw it to the cat. Add another blob of butter and stir a bit more. Pile it out on top of the fried bread you remembered to make before you started on the eggs. Cover with slices of smoked salmon, add some pepper, pour yourself a stiff scotch and water and away you go! Cheers!

I used to feel sorry for Robin Hood. All that bother with the sherriff of Nottingham just to get a joint of game that would, when roasted, turn out to be a grey, dry, stringy, and thoroughly unappetising meat. I imagine they sat round their fire in the greenwood glade miserably chewing venison chunks and dreaming of succulent roast beef or juicy pork with lots of crackling! At Grey Gables we serve this special recipe, which might sound rather disgusting but in fact it turns venison into the superb classic dinner dish everyone believes it to be.

Fillet of venison 'Grey Gables'

1 oz butter
$1\frac{1}{2}$ lb fillet of venison
1 onion, finely diced
1 dessertspoon French mustard
5 tablespoons plus 1 capful of gin
30 good quality black cherries
$\frac{1}{4}$ pint sour cream
Freshly ground salt and pepper

Cut the venison into half-inch slices and marinade for at least 2 hours (but preferably overnight) in the 5 tablespoons of gin. When ready to cook, pat the meat dry. Melt the butter and sauté the onion. Add the venison and cook for about 5 minutes. Add the mustard and freshly ground salt and pepper and cook for a further 5 minutes, lowering the heat if necessary. Add the cherries, bottled or tinned, and the capful of gin. Stir well in for about a minute, then add the sour cream and simmer for about 15 minutes. Check seasoning before serving.

Ever since they began the change to organic farming at Bridge Farm, Pat Archer has been more and more concerned over the sort of food that her family eats. First she cut down on the amount of dairy produce, then she started avoiding food with additives, then she put the entire household (including Bessie the dog) on a high-fibre diet. The revolt only came after she announced: 'No more tins of baked beans – they've got too much sugar in them! I'm going to prepare wholesome homemade beans in future.' Next morning Johnny was discovered halfway to Blossom Hill Cottage, his belongings in a bag over his shoulder, searching for his 'Grandma Peggy' who would give him crisps, and shop cakes, and *proper* baked beans on toast.

Pat was bewildered. 'But my baked beans are so much nicer!' she exclaimed, 'you think my beans are nicer, don't you, Tony?' Tony mumbled and gargled incoherently for a bit, then his face brightened. 'They're pretty revolting on toast,' he said, 'but terrific in that pork thing you left in the oven the other night – you remember, when I got held up at the Bull by Uncle Walter and you went off to your women's group party in Borchester.' Pat later gave me the recipe for her pork and bean supper dish.

Crispy pork and haricot bean casserole

Line a casserole dish with the bacon. Drain and rinse the beans and place in a large bowl. Add all the other ingredients to the beans, except the pork. Stir well and pour over the bacon in the casserole dish. Make a nest of the pork joint and add it, skin side up. Tightly seal the casserole, using foil if necessary, and cook for 150°C (300°F, gas mark 2) for 4 hours. Remove the lid and turn up the heat to 220°C (425°F, gas mark 7) for another 30-40 minutes to make nice crackling. If the beans seem to be drying up in the last few minutes, add a tablespoonful of hot water. This dish can be made in advance and then reheated.

2 lb lean pork with skin to crackle

5 rashers streaky bacon, derinded

$\frac{1}{2}$ lb dried haricot beans soaked overnight in cold water

12 oz carton chopped or puréed tomatoes (*not* tomato purée)

Freshly ground salt and pepper

3-4 leaves of basil, finely chopped

1 sprig of thyme

2 teaspoons demerara sugar

The orchard at Grange Farm is mainly filled with cider-apple trees, including one that yields the famous Kingston Black, but there are a couple of Bramley trees which were planted when Clarrie and Eddie became engaged (it's a Borsetshire custom to plant a fruit tree on any notable date), and which now provide enough fruit for apple pies and for these mouth-watering oat and apple cakes. 'Every time I make them I think back to the day Eddie asked me to be his wife,' says Clarrie fondly, 'and how I gave him my life-savings so he could make a hit record and become famous.' Well, Eddie's still making records and Clarrie's still making oat cakes – and I know which of the two I would vote a hit!

Clarrie Grundy's oat and apple cake

8 oz self-raising flour
8 oz oats
4 oz butter
2 heaped tablespoons golden syrup (approx 8 oz)
2 Bramleys, peeled and diced
2 oz raisins (optional)
2 oz sultanas (optional)

Melt the butter and syrup together over a low heat. Sift the flour into the mix and stir well in. Gradually add the oats and keep stirring until thoroughly mixed. Add the apple and dried fruit. Put the mixture in a greased Swiss-roll tin, 11 by 7 inches, and level the surface with the back of a knife. Cook in a preheated oven at 180°C (350°F, gas mark 4) for half an hour.

It's a chilly, wet November afternoon with sheep huddled against the dripping hedge-rows, birds hunched on the swaying branches, and cows moving uneasily as wind and rain gust under the cowshed door. The kitchen at Brookfield, though, is brightly lit, beautifully warm from the Aga, and has its blinds pulled firmly down against the nasty weather outside. Jill is happily delving into her cupboards sorting out ingredients, while Elizabeth is sitting at the table pretending to revise for an essay and absently eating glacé cherries. David comes in, having abandoned ploughing, and demands a mug of tea. He pinches some cherries while he waits, and a minute later Phil comes in from the office muttering about a difficult calving and goodness knows what Jethro's doing at Hollowtree, and he gobbles up a few cherries and suddenly Jill wails, 'Stop it, all of you! I had half a pound of cherries there and now there isn't a single one left!' Then David has to run down to Martha's for some more cherries, and Elizabeth is shouted at for nibbling the chopped almonds – and the Brookfield Christmas pudding is eventually made! It's a fruity pudding which uses strong barley wine instead of the more usual milk or beer.

A plum pudding with barley wine

In a bowl mix up the flour, suet, sugar, breadcrumbs, salt and mixed spice. Chop the cherries and add to the bowl with the nuts, dried fruit and candied peel, mixing thoroughly. Make a well in the mixture and add the beaten eggs, barley wine, and the juice and rind of the orange and lemon. Mix to a soft consistency – you might have to add more liquid at this stage. Cover and allow to stand for a few hours. Grease two 2-pint basins or four 1-pint basins, and fill to the top with the mixture. Cover with foil and steam for at least 6 hours. Remove the foil and allow to cool. Store covered with clean foil. At Christmas resteam the pudding for 2 hours before eating.

$\frac{1}{2}$ lb raisins
$\frac{3}{4}$ lb sultanas
$\frac{3}{4}$ lb currants
$\frac{1}{4}$ lb candied peel
2 oz chopped almonds
2 oz glacé cherries
$\frac{1}{2}$ lb soft brown sugar
$\frac{1}{2}$ lb breadcrumbs
4 oz self-raising flour
$\frac{1}{2}$ lb suet
Grated rind and juice of 1 lemon and 1 orange
1 teaspoon mixed spice
$\frac{1}{2}$ teaspoon salt
5 eggs
$\frac{1}{2}$ bottle strong barley wine

There is nothing Jethro Larkin likes better, so he tells me, than a dollop of pear chutney with his bread and cheese. 'My mother Mabel was a great chutney-maker in her time,' he adds, 'and her pear chutney had a reputation t'other side of Borbury. I don't know why she didn't sell it in jars with her name on the front. We could have made a fortune like Worcester sauce has, and all had Rolls Royce cars to ride round in. Me, Clarrie, and one for Rosie and Denis in Yarmouth.' 'What about Martha Woodford's pear chutney?' I ask, trying to find him a silver lining. 'Goooor!' says Jethro, and curls his lip in scorn. 'You know what Martha Woodford puts in her pear chutney?' He leans towards me over his beer mug. 'Garlic!'

In the shop next day Martha breaks down under heavy questioning and confesses that Jethro is quite right, she does use garlic in her pear chutney. 'But Mabel Larkin did just the same,' she says indignantly, 'in fact it was her who gave me the recipe!'

Pear chutney

4 lb Conference pears

1 lb onions, peeled

1 lb tomatoes, peeled

2 green peppers, deseeded

$\frac{1}{2}$ lb raisins

1 lb demerara sugar

2 cloves garlic, crushed

$\frac{1}{8}$ level teaspoon cayenne pepper

1 level tablespoon ground ginger

$1\frac{1}{2}$ pints malt or pickling vinegar

6 whole cloves

1 level tablespoon pickling spice

$\frac{1}{2}$ oz salt

Peel, core and finely chop the pears. Finely chop the onions, tomatoes and peppers. Place in a preserving pan or large saucepan. Cover and cook gently without any extra liquid for about 20 minutes. Add all the remaining ingredients with the cloves and pickling spice tied in muslin. Heat gently until the chutney becomes thick, stirring occasionally to prevent sticking. This will take about $1\frac{1}{2}$ hours. Remove the muslin bag, spoon the chutney into pots, and cover with vinegar-proof covers. Label and store in a cool, dry place for at least 2 weeks before use.

December

RECIPES FOR DECEMBER

Chestnut soup

Cauliflower cheese with yoghurt and walnuts

Betty Tucker's chilli beef with beans

Rich oxtail and cider casserole

Roast veal with devilled pears

Christmas pheasant with cream and apples

Jack Woolley's Old English trifle

Debbie Macy's cheese and anchovy fingers

Brown bread ice-cream

DECEMBER NOTEBOOK

Yellow gorse is in bloom, and so is groundsel, and red deadnettle is covered in dusky-pink snapdragon flowers. Martha Woodford collects them, together with garden violets, and makes small posies of winter flowers to sell at the Playgroup Christmas Fayre in the village hall. Another stall sells variegated holly from Brookfield, thick with shiny berries, bunches of mistletoe from the orchard at Grange Farm, and pine cones sprayed with silver and gold.

The three great evergreens of Christmas are believed to have magic powers. Holly repels witches, circlets of ivy will keep fairies and hobgoblins away from cattle and stop them from stealing the milk, and mistletoe improves the crop of any orchard it favours. Joe Grundy regards it as a sign of divine grace that his old orchard is so blessed, but Tom is scornful. 'It's a very sticky berry is mistletoe,' he says, 'and when birds have had a feed they look for a tree to wipe their beaks on. That's how the seed gets spread – it's nothing to do with miracles.' Joe Grundy grins in triumph. 'Maybe, but why do the little birds wipe their beaks on *my* trees, eh? What makes them come all the way to Grange Farm instead of wiping their beaks on your pear tree, Tom Forrest? You answer me that!'

The south-facing wall of the coachhouse is covered with ivy, now bearing rich green blossoms. A mild, sunny day brings out two bluebottles, a wasp, and a bedraggled-looking butterfly. They have moved on here from the tattered purple flowers of the Michaelmas daisy; end-of-season revellers seeking a last sip of nectar and assuring each other that it isn't really time to go home. Soon it will be too late. The first snows will come, and they will be dead.

Apart from foolish pleasure-seekers, everything is asleep that can be. Toads have buried themselves in rotting leaves, frogs have burrowed into the muddy bottoms of pools, the dormouse is curled up in his nest, paws firmly covering his whiskers and nose, and the bats in St Stephen's belfry are deep in slumber.

Of animals that are awake, the fox is the most active, for this is the mating season, when vixens are coming on heat and dog foxes travel miles to find them. The call of the dog fox, and the vixen's reply, sound out eerily on the still, frosty night. The lovesick dog fox is known as a 'traveller' to the hunt, and is much appreciated because he does not know the local territory. If put out of cover he is likely to set his mask for a more distant earth – and give much better sport!

A sudden snap of icy weather brings birds crowding to Elizabeth's birdtable in search of food. First a robin and a great tit, the robin trying to frighten the tit by displaying his red breast, and the tit setting his wings and tail fluttering aggressively in reply. Then a blackbird alights, and coal tits carry crumbs away to hide in a secret place. For a while the birds eat together amicably, then four starlings – the shiny black hells angels of the bird world – descend and frighten everyone else off. Elizabeth runs out in a fury and throws rotting apples at them, and the starlings wheel and swoop in alarm before disappearing behind the barn. Soon robins and tits return to the birdtable, and blackbirds peck happily at the rotting apples. It's really no wonder that starlings are so ill-tempered.

RECIPES FOR DECEMBER

There are (I was taught at Lausanne) three items of tinned food that a good cook is allowed to use without inviting shame and everlasting dishonour. These are tinned anchovies, tinned tomatoes and tomato purée, and tinned unsweetened chestnut purée. Fresh chestnuts are hard to get hold of anyway, except during December, and even then I prefer to reserve them for roasting in the fire or stuffing inside the festive turkey.

If you want to make a soup with fresh chestnuts, mind you, it is easily done. Put the chestnuts in cold water and bring to the boil. Shell and skin them. Simmer them until cooked in a good stock with chopped celery and carrots. Take out the chestnuts and sieve or blend them. Strain the stock. Put the chestnut purée back. Reheat and serve with a little cream and sherry added. The most important thing is to use a good, home-made stock, and that is much easier than it used to be when cooks had to mess about boiling up stock-pots every couple of days. Now it is simple to make a stock, pour into half-pint containers, and use from the freezer as needed.

Here is a chestnut soup recipe using one of the permitted tins.

Chestnut soup

Melt the butter in a large saucepan. Add the onion and carrot and fry gently until they start to brown. Add the chestnut purée, then the stock, together with the mace and bay leaf. Season. Bring slowly to the boil, then simmer for one hour. Take off the heat and liquidise. Before serving add the sherry, reheat, and swirl in the cream.

1 carrot, sliced

1 onion, chopped

1 oz butter

1 tin (usually $15\frac{1}{2}$ oz) unsweetened chestnut purée

$1\frac{1}{2}$ pints good stock (pheasant stock is wonderful)

Freshly ground salt and pepper

Blade of mace

1 bay leaf

3 tablespoons cream

2 tablespoons dry sherry

Tony is off to the Borchester Fatstock Show for the afternoon ('You ought to come, Caroline,' he says, 'the auctioneers hand out whisky and big fat cigars') and Pat and I are going Christmas shopping in Felpersham, so I am invited for a spot of early lunch at Bridge Farm. Pat cooks cauliflower cheese and Tony comes in from washing down the dairy and says, 'Goodie, goodie, lots of gammon for me, love,' and Pat says, 'There isn't any gammon, we eat far too much meat,' and Tony's mouth drops open in shock. 'We *always* have gammon and tinned tomatoes with cauliflower cheese!' he says indignantly. 'Not this time, Tony,' says Pat. 'This time we're having it with live yoghurt and walnuts. I'll re-educate this family's eating habits if it kills me.' Tony, and Tommy, and Helen, eat in stunned silence (as would John, no doubt, if he were present) and are polite only because I am there.

Poor Pat! Cauliflower is not my favourite vegetable, and I normally only eat it raw and crunchy with a garlic dip, but this really is a very tasty light lunch dish, and perfect for using up the last of the autumn cauliflowers.

Cauliflower cheese with yoghurt and walnuts

1 large cauliflower
1 oz butter
1 tablespoon cornflour
5 oz natural live yoghurt
2 oz grated parmesan cheese
1 oz grated stilton cheese
Freshly ground salt and pepper
4 oz chopped walnuts (and whole nuts for garnish)

Steam the cauliflower lightly. While still crisp put in a separate dish and keep warm. To make the sauce melt the butter and mix in the cornflour, salt and pepper. Then mix in the yoghurt and cheese. Heat, stirring well, until the sauce thickens, but be careful not to boil. Mix in the chopped nuts. Pour the sauce over the cauliflower. Garnish with whole nuts and serve immediately.

A murky, winter's evening at Grange Farm. To frighten away burglars a solitary light bulb is slung over the barn door on an extension cable. From the turkey shed comes a constant, low, discontented gobbling noise. Suddenly the back door of the farmhouse opens and in a shaft of light appears a strange and wonderful figure wearing soft-tanned leather boots, a bootlace tie, a cowboy hat with polished horns, and a waistcoat sparkling with blue and purple glitter. 'Have a nice evening, ma'am,' says the figure as I pass inside to talk to Clarrie, 'and take care how you go, you hear?' A moment later Eddie Grundy, the megastar who beat Wayne Tucson the singing oilman from Hollerton to the top of the *Borchester Echo* pop ratings, climbs into his powder-blue Ford Capri with its leopard-skin seats, stuffed-ferret brake lights, and swinging CB aerial, and is on his way to the Borchester Country and Western talent night.

Mike Tucker, the Ambridge milkman, is a keen country music fan. He and his wife Betty recently organised a 'Country Evening' at the village hall, and for supper Betty cooked up a vast tureen of minced beef with bacon and beans. It was a wonderfully warm and comforting meal for a cold night, and although Eddie had demanded charcoal-grilled steaks all evening he soon finished off his beef 'n' beans and tried to sneak into the queue for second helpings. As Betty didn't go to *cordon bleu* cookery school in Lausanne she doesn't have to worry about using tinned beans!

Betty Tucker's chilli beef with beans

In a good casserole dish that can be used on top of the stove gently fry the onion and bacon. Add a little oil or butter if necessary. When browned add the mince, turn up the heat and fry, turning energetically, until the beef is also browned. Mix in a dessertspoon of chilli powder. Tip in the tin of beans and stir everything up. Move to the oven, cover and cook for about an hour at 200°C (400°F, gas mark 6). Serve with jacket potatoes and sprouts.

1 onion, roughly chopped
3 rashers bacon, also chopped
A little oil or butter for frying
1½ lb minced beef
15 oz tin of baked beans (plus a small tin if you like beans)
Chilli powder

At Brookfield the main calving period of the year is now drawing to a close. About a hundred cows calve between September and the end of the year, but unfortunately for David they don't come once a day at a regular time! More often than not he and Phil are out in the cowshed worrying over a difficult birth just as Jill is dishing up supper in the kitchen. 'I've given up cooking food that won't wait,' she says. 'Every autumn we live on chops that can be cooked while the men are washing or casseroles that will keep for hours.'

This oxtail casserole is made with cider and jellied veal and is a great Brookfield favourite. According to David, the longer it is kept gently cooking in the Aga the better it gets.

Rich oxtail and cider casserole

2 tablespoons olive oil

2 oz butter

6 oz onions, roughly chopped

6 oz carrots, roughly chopped

2 lb oxtail

2 tablespoons seasoned flour

4 oz jellied veal or tongue, chopped

$\frac{3}{4}$ pint cider

$\frac{3}{4}$ pint good brown stock

1 teaspoon crushed juniper berries

1 clove garlic, crushed

2 sprigs of fresh thyme

3 bay leaves

6 oz button onions

8 oz button mushrooms

Freshly ground salt and pepper

Melt the oil and half the butter in a flameproof casserole. Sauté the vegetables for 3 to 4 minutes on a high heat. Keep them on the move while cooking. Remove excess fat from the oxtail and toss in the seasoned flour until well coated. Fry the oxtail until golden brown. Add the jellied veal or tongue. Add the cider and stock – enough to cover the meat. Add the juniper berries, garlic, thyme and bay leaves. Put on the lid and cook at 130°C (250°F, gas mark $\frac{1}{2}$) for 4 hours. Cool and refrigerate overnight. Bring to room temperature, remove the fat and reheat for 2 hours at 130°C (250°F, gas mark $\frac{1}{2}$). Sauté the button onions and mushrooms in remaining butter and add to the casserole for the last half hour, cooking without the lid. Season to taste.

On my first Christmas in Ambridge Jennifer gave a dinner party for eight at Home Farm, and I was invited along as Shula's friend, and experienced the amazing warmth and hospitality of Ambridge village life. It was Christmas Eve, there were huge bunches of holly round the oak-beamed fireplace, and even though there were five women to three men Brian gallantly kissed us all (all the women that is) under the mistletoe, watched by giggling children from the top of the stairs. We ate a delicious and very festive dish of roast veal with devilled pears, and whenever I have eaten it since I have remembered that wonderful evening at Home Farm. This is the recipe for eight, as used that night by Jennifer.

Roast veal with devilled pears

Unroll the veal joint. Cut 8 oz of veal from the inside of the joint. Mince or finely chop this portion. Melt half the butter in a large saucepan. Add the onion and cook for a few minutes until soft. Remove from the heat and allow to cool slightly. Stir in the minced veal, chopped watercress, cinnamon, breadcrumbs, hazelnuts, orange rind, salt and eggs. Mix well. Using floured hands, roll half the stuffing into 16 balls and set aside. Spread the remaining stuffing on the inside of the meat. Re-roll the joint and tie with string. Place the joint, with the opening underneath, in a large foil-lined roasting pan. Cover with foil and roast in the centre of a preheated oven at 220°C (425°F, gas mark 7) for $1\frac{3}{4}$ hours. Mix the honey, vinegar and mustard together in a dish. Peel, halve and core the pears. Cut a thin slice off the rounded side of each pear half so that it will lie flat. Add the halves to the honey marinade and cover the dish. Remove the roasting pan from the oven, pour off the juices and reserve for gravy. Place the pears round the joint in the pan and add a stuffing ball to each pear cavity. Spoon the honey marinade over the joint and the pears. Return to the oven and cook, uncovered, for a further 40 minutes. Remove the string and carve the joint in thick slices. Arrange the slices, and the pears, on a heated serving dish. Pour the pan juices, together with the reserved juice, into a measuring jug. Make up to 1 pint with vegetable water and pour into a saucepan. Cream the remaining butter and the flour together to make *beurre manie*, and add to the pan. Whisk over a moderate heat until thick, then pour into a warmed gravy boat. Garnish the serving dish with orange slices and watercress.

4 lb shoulder veal joint

2 oz butter

1 large onion, peeled and finely chopped

1 bunch watercress, chopped

1 teaspoon ground cinnamon

6 oz fresh breadcrumbs

2 oz hazelnuts, chopped

1 dessertspoon grated orange rind

$\frac{1}{2}$ teaspoon salt

2 eggs, beaten

4 tablespoons clear honey

4 tablespoons red wine vinegar

1 tablespoon made English mustard

8 fresh pears

1 oz plain flour

Sliced fresh orange and water-cress for garnish

The courtyard is full of shiny Range Rovers, Jaguars, MG Montego Estates and 'Mercs'; Tom and George strut proudly about in their best thornproof jackets and breeches; a bevy of beaters jump up and down to keep their toes warm; Higgs has abandoned his game of poker in the greenhouse and tugs his forelock to every 'gun' he thinks will give him a massive tip; and in the kitchen Trudy Porter busily fills flasks with game soup laced with sherry. For this is the day of the Christmas shoot, the high spot of the Grey Gables sporting year.

After today only cock pheasants will be in danger, while hen pheasants will be caught and put in laying pens. This might seem hard on the cock pheasants, but there are generally far too many of them left by this time in the season. They are cunning, devious birds, you see, and despite their size and brilliant, beautiful plumage they are much better at dodging the guns than the dowdy, trusting, and scatter-brained females. Cock pheasants are also over-sexed and quarrelsome, and they knock each other about and distress the hens so much that the poor birds wander off into the woods alone and become infertile. So, from now until the end of January the cock pheasants will be regarded as fair game, but the hen pheasants will be safe – providing, of course, that they don't wander over the river to Grange Farm land. When it comes to potting something for supper the Grundies have no respect for sex, age or religion.

Pheasants should be allowed to hang for four or five days (in average seasonal weather) to develop the flavour. Anyone who boasts that pheasant is nothing until the flesh turns green is asking for food poisoning. Early in the season there is nothing so nice as a plump, tender hen pheasant simply roast and served with game chips, bread sauce, crumbled, crispy bacon and a port-wine gravy. But cock pheasants are not quite as tender and sweet, and I prefer them cooked in a delicious apple and cream casserole.

Christmas pheasant with cream and apples

Season the pheasant with salt and pepper. Heat the butter and oil in a casserole and brown the pheasant evenly all over. Remove the pheasant and sauté the mushrooms for 30 seconds. Add the apples to the pan and replace the pheasant. Pour over the white wine, replace the lid and cook at 180°C (350°F, gas mark 4) for 1 hour. When the bird is ready, remove it to a warm dish. Heat the casserole until most of the liquid has evaporated, and then stir in the cream. Heat gently, season to taste, and then pour the sauce over the pheasant. Garnish with watercress.

(NOTE: A good-sized cock pheasant will just about feed four people, but if you're all going to be hungry it might be wise to substitute two hen pheasants, and increase the other ingredients a little bit.)

1 pheasant
1 tablespoon butter
1 tablespoon oil
2 oz mushrooms, thinly sliced
$\frac{1}{2}$ lb Cox's apples, peeled, cored and thinly sliced
$\frac{1}{4}$ pint white wine
$\frac{1}{4}$ pint double cream
Freshly ground salt and pepper
Watercress for garnish

Mr Woolley stares in horror at the sweet trolley. The brandysnap gâteau is eyed with scorn; the crème brûlé is dismissed in anger, no matter how crunchy the topping and custardy the inside; the creamy hazelnut roulade is beneath contempt. 'What I want to know, Caroline,' he says in a voice trembling with indignation, 'is where's the Old English Trifle?' Just then the chef in person, the great Jean Paul, brings one in from the kitchen . . . a huge bowl of raspberry sponge, brandy, sherry, white wine, double-rich custard, cream, syllabub, and crystallised orange, lemon, and chestnuts. 'Christmas just isn't Christmas without an Old English trifle,' says Mr Woolley happily, and the Christmas houseparty guests relax back into a glazed torpor, already stuffed to bursting on turkey, plum pudding and cake.

Jack Woolley's Old English trifle

10 sponge cakes

3 tablespoons brandy

¼ pint white wine

1 carton Kathy Holland's raspberry freezer jam or 4 heaped tablespoons ordinary raspberry jam

1 pint single cream

2 eggs, beaten

2 eggs yolks, beaten

1 heaped tablespoon sugar

Break the sponge cakes into the bottom of a large trifle dish. Spoon over the brandy and as much wine as the sponge will take. Press down with the back of a spoon and spread the jam over the top. Put the cream into a saucepan and heat gently to just under boiling point. Stir in the eggs and yolks and beat well. Heat steadily (in a double saucepan if you wish) but keep below boiling point. Stir until the sauce thickens. Resist the temptation to speed things up, or it will curdle. When thickened, stir in the sugar until it dissolves. Allow to cool completely before pouring over the sponge. Refrigerate overnight. Top with old-fashioned syllabub and decorate with crystallised orange and lemon segments and crystallised chestnuts (or blanched almonds).

Syllabub

¼ pint white wine (not too dry)

1 tablespoon medium sherry

2 tablespoons brandy

1 lemon

2 oz caster sugar

½ pint double cream

Leave the wine, sherry and brandy to stand for about 4 hours with the thinly cut peel of the lemon (make sure there's no white pith on it). Drain to remove the peel, then stir in the sugar. Add the cream and whisk to the soft peak stage. Spread over the trifle and leave, chilled, for 2 hours before decorating.

In the week before Christmas there are usually two parties held in the village hall – one for the playgroup, and the other for the over-sixties. The vicar's wife, Dorothy, helps at both and swears she can't tell the difference between them. Pat Archer, who also helps at both, disagrees. 'The over-sixties are a lot nippier at musical chairs,' she says, 'and generally speaking they don't splat their jelly and ice-cream on the walls.' Both parties, though, greatly appreciate Debbie's cheese and anchovy fingers, even if they do have a tendency to ask for them with Marmite spread. Back at Home Farm Debbie (who is becoming *very* sophisticated now she's at Cheltenham) serves these fingers with a special sherry dip.

Debbie Macy's cheese and anchovy fingers

6 oz plain flour
Salt
2 oz butter
4 oz cheddar cheese, grated
2 level teaspoons anchovy essence

Sieve the flour and salt into a basin. Rub in butter until the mixture resembles fine breadcrumbs. Stir in the grated cheese. Bind together with anchovy essence and enough water to form a stiff dough. Turn on to a floured board, and roll out to a rectangle about 9 by 5 inches. Cut into fingers ½ by 2½-inches long. Place on greased baking sheets and bake in a moderate oven at 170°C (325°F, gas mark 3) for 20 minutes, until crisp and golden brown.

Sherry dip

6 oz butter
12 oz cheddar, finely grated
1 level tablespoon caster sugar
Pinch of cayenne pepper
6 tablespoons sherry

Cream the butter and beat in the grated cheese. Add the sugar, cayenne pepper, and sherry. Beat together to give a soft consistency.

Walking through the silent, sleeping woods at the year's end, I am startled by a woodcock rising from under my feet with a flurry of beating wings. The woodcock, no doubt, is even more startled than I am. They are strange, mysterious birds. Some of them migrate to Ireland or Scandinavia, others stay here all the year round. There seems no reason or logic behind it, other than a preference, or not, for winter holidays.

They are golden brown, and beautiful, and very solitary, spending most of the day alone, crouched on the ground and watching the world go by. At dusk they fly long distances to their feeding ground.

I watch my woodcock wheel slowly over the lake towards the setting winter's sun. Then I turn back to Grey Gables. Tomorrow will be a new year, but tonight I have an old friend coming to supper. There is a plump hen pheasant ready to go in the oven, and I have made his favourite pudding – brown bread ice-cream with apricot sauce.

Brown bread ice-cream

6 oz stoneground wholemeal breadcrumbs, not too fine

$\frac{1}{2}$ pint double cream

$\frac{1}{2}$ pint single cream

4 oz soft brown sugar

2 eggs, separated

1 tablespoon Tia Maria (or rum)

Grill the breadcrumbs under a medium heat until crisp. Keep them on the move with a wooden spoon to ensure that they do not become hard or too brown. Whip the cream with the sugar to the soft peak stage. Beat the egg yolks with the Tia Maria and stir into the cream. Fold in the breadcrumbs. Pour into a container and cover. Freeze for an hour. Whisk the egg whites until stiff. Return the ice-cream to a bowl and stir thoroughly. Fold in the egg whites and cover again. Return to the freezer for at least 2 hours. Place in the fridge at least half an hour before serving.

Apricot sauce

4 heaped tablespoons of good quality apricot jam

2 tablespoons sugar

6-8 tablespoons white wine

Heat the jam gently with the sugar and wine, stirring all the time until a smooth texture is achieved. You can sieve it, if you wish, to get rid of the apricot skins, but this is not really necessary.

INDEX

Almond shortbreads, Elizabeth's 82
Apple and pork-liver pâté 102
Apple, blackberry and almond pie
   131
Apple sauce 115
Apricot sauce 158

Bacon soup with dumplings 38
Bean crock, Jersey 54
Bean salad, French 89
Beans, green with parmesan and
   chives 100
Beef
   A famous beef stew with prunes
      14
   Betty Tucker's chilli beef with
      beans 151
   Pot-roasted brisket with root
      vegetables 40
   Rich oxtail and cider casserole 152
Biscuits, wholewheat orange 32
Blackberry jelly, Jennifer's spiced
   120
Brandied chocolate pots, Lord
   Netherbourne's 18
Brandied orange cider syllabub 57
Bread-and-butter pudding, spiced 70
Brisket, pot-roasted with root
   vegetables 40
Brown bread ice-cream 158
Brussels sprouts with chestnuts 137
Buns, cinnamon 18

Cake
   Borsetshire 'Heysel' cake 81
   Clarrie Grundy's oat and apple cake
      142
   Old-fashioned lemon curdcake
      105
   Raspberry pavlova cake 94
   Rhubarb hot cake 44
Carrot pudding, baked 56
Cauliflower cheese with yoghurt and
   walnuts 150
Champagne, elderflower 82
Cheese
   Borsetshire cheese and crab soup
      64
   Cauliflower cheese with yoghurt
      and walnuts 150

Debbie Macy's cheese and
   anchovy fingers 157
Green beans with parmesan and
   thyme 100
Stilton and apples in flaky pastry
   127
Cherry and hazelnut crumble 93
Cherry batter pudding, Trudy
   Porter's 92
Chestnut soup 149
Chicken
   Chicken-liver and green pepper-
      corn pâté 66
   Lemon roast chicken with garlic
      27
   Nelson's chicken-liver pâté 12
   Sugar peas with bacon and
      chicken livers 88
Chilli beef with beans, Betty
   Tucker's 151
Chocolate pots, Lord Nether-
   bourne's brandied 18
Chutney, pear 144
Cinnamon buns 18
Cinnamon gooseberry pie,
   Christine Barford's 69
Cod and bacon supper, Bill Insley's
   26
Courgette and mushroom salad 129
Crab, hot, and mushrooms 112
Crock, Jersey bean 54
Curried parsnip soup, Colonel
   Danby's 23

Duck
   Crispy roast duck with orange
   sauce 91
   Duck roasted with wine and
      pears 41

Egg
   Loxley leek and egg flan 13
   Nigel's scrambled eggs with
      smoked salmon 140
   Plaice with egg and prawn sauce
      51
   Tomato, egg and anchovy salad
      99
Elizabethan pork hot-pot 68

Fingers, Debbie Macy's cheese and
   anchovy 157
Fish
   Baked leeks with prawns and
      walnuts 25
   Bill Insley's cod and bacon supper
      26
   Borsetshire cheese and crab soup
      64
   Buttered salmon steaks in white
      wine 63

Debbie Macy's cheese and
   anchovy fingers 157
Hot crab and mushrooms 112
Nigel's scrambled eggs with
   smoked salmon 140
Plaice with egg and prawn sauce
   51
Salmon and asparagus in pastry
   77
Tomato, egg and anchovy salad
   99
Flan, Loxley leek and egg 13
Freezer jam, Kathy Holland's 106

Game
   Christmas pheasant with cream
      and apples 155
   Eddie Grundy's harvest rabbit
      casserole 113
   Fillet of venison 'Grey Gables'
      140
   Game pie 28
   Pigeon breasts in red wine with
      gooseberry sauce 130
   Roasted guineafowl stuffed with
      grapes 16
Gammon steaks with sour cream
   and cucumber 53
Ginger pears 132
Goose, roast Michaelmas, with
   potato stuffing 114
Gooseberry pie, Christine Barford's
   cinnamon 69
Guineafowl, roasted, stuffed with
   grapes 16

Haricot bean casserole, crispy pork
   and 141
Harvest soup, Ambridge 126
Hazelnut and Marsala ice-cream 132
Herb sauce 78
'Heysel' cake, Borsetshire 81

Ice-cream
   Brown bread 158
   Hazelnut and Marsala 132

Jersey bean crock 54

Kebabs
   Lamb with herbs 104
   Lamb with yoghurt 104
   Pork with courgettes 104
Kidneys, the Colonel's lambs', with
   redcurrant jelly 55

Lamb
   English lamb with asparagus 76
   Lamb kebabs with herbs 104
   Lamb kebabs with yoghurt 104
   Rosemary roast lamb 67

The Colonel's lambs' kidneys
  with redcurrant jelly 55
Leek and bacon pie, Edgeley 138
Leek and egg flan, Loxley 13
Leek and parsnip soup 24
Leeks, baked with prawns and
  walnuts 25
Lemon curdcake, old-fashioned 105
Lentil soup, rosemary and 11

Marjoram casserole, Marjorie's 37
Mushroom sauce 102
Mushrooms, deep-fried stuffed 66

Nigel's scrambled eggs with smoked
  salmon 140

Oat and apple cake, Clarrie
  Grundy's 142
Onion and apple sauce 67
Onion sauce 115
Orange biscuits, wholewheat 32
Oxtail, rich, and cider casserole
  152

Pancakes, strawberry and peppercorn
  80
Parsnip soup, Colonel Danby's
  curried 23
Pastry
  Jean-Paul's shortcrust pastry 57
  Pork fillet in pastry with mush-
    room sauce 101
  Salmon and asparagus in pastry 77
  Special suet crust pastry 46
  Stilton and apples in flaky pastry
    127
  Stuffed sugar plum pastries 117

Pâté
  Apple and pork-liver pâté 102
  Chicken-liver and green pepper-
    corn pâté 66
  Nelson's chicken-liver pâté 12
Pavlova cake, raspberry 94
Pear and almond tart 118
Pear chutney 144
Pears, ginger 132
Pheasant, Christmas, with cream and
  apples 155
Pie
  Apple, blackberry and almond pie
    131
  Christine Barford's cinnamon
    gooseberry pie 69
  Edgeley leek and bacon pie 138
  Game pie 28
Pigeon breasts in red wine with
  gooseberry sauce 130
Plaice with egg and prawn sauce 51
Plough Monday pudding 17

Plum pastries, stuffed sugar 117
Plum pudding with barley wine 143
Plum soup, chilled 87
Potatoes
  Hot potato salad 116
  New potatoes in lemon sauce 65
  Sugar-browned new potatoes 65
Pork
  Apple and pork-liver pâté 102
  Crispy pork and haricot bean
    casserole 141
  Elizabethan pork hot-pot 68
  Fillets of pork with apricots 42
  Jersey bean crock 54
  Pork fillet in pastry with mush-
    room sauce 101
  Roast hand of pork with water-
    cress stuffing 128
Puddings
  Baked carrot pudding 56
  Jill Archer's Sussex Pond pudding
    45
  Plough Monday pudding 17
  Plum pudding with barley wine
    143
  Spiced bread-and-butter pudding
    70
  Toffee upside-down pudding 31
  Trudy Porter's cherry batter
    pudding 92

Rabbit casserole, Eddie Grundy's
  harvest 113
Raspberry pavlova cake 94
Rhubarb and orange lattice tart 43
Rhubarb hot cake 44
Rosemary and lentil soup 11

Salad
  Courgette and mushroom salad
    129
  French bean salad 89
  Hot potato salad 116
  Spring salad 52
  Tomato, egg and anchovy salad
    99
Salmon and asparagus in pastry 77
Salmon steaks in white wine,
  buttered 63
Sauces
  Apple sauce 115
  Apricot sauce 158
  Egg and prawn sauce 51
  Herb sauce 78
  Mushroom sauce 102
  Onion and apple sauce 67
  Onion sauce 115
Scones, Borbury fruited tea 106
Sherry dip 157
Shortbread, Elizabeth's almond 82
Shortcrust pastry, Jean-Paul's 57

Soups
  Ambridge harvest soup 126
  Bacon soup with dumplings 38
  Borsetshire cheese and crab soup
    64
  Chestnut soup 149
  Chilled plum soup 87
  Colonel Danby's curried parsnip
    soup 23
  Leek and parsnip soup 24
  Rosemary and lentil soup 11
  Tomato, orange and tarragon
    soup 111
  Verdant watercress soup 75
  Victorian sprout and ham soup
    139
Spring salad 52
Sprout and ham soup, Victorian 139
Sprouts, Brussels, with chestnuts 137
Stilton and apples in flaky pastry 127
Strawberry and peppercorn
  pancakes 80
Strawberry tartlets, Jean-Paul's 79
Stuffed sugar plum pastries 117
Suet crust pastry, special 46
Sugar peas with bacon and chicken
  livers 88
Sussex Pond pudding, Jill Archer's
  45
Syllabub 156
Syllabub, brandied orange cider 57

Tarts
  Jean-Paul's strawberry tartlets 79
  Pear and almond tart 118
  Rhubarb and orange lattice tart
    43
  Treacle tart 59
Toffee upside-down pudding 31
Tomato, egg and anchovy salad 99
Tomato, orange and tarragon soup
  111
Treacle tart 59
Trifle, Jack Woolley's Old English
  156
Turnips, Jethro Larkin's crisp-topped
  39

Veal
  Churcham stuffed loin of veal 90
  Roast veal with devilled pears 153
Venison, fillet of, 'Grey Gables' 140
Victorian sprout and ham soup 139

Watercress soup, verdant 75